CONTEMPORARY AMERICAN POETRY:
A Checklist

by
LLOYD DAVIS
and
ROBERT IRWIN

The Scarecrow Press, Inc.
Metuchen, N.J.   1975

Library of Congress Cataloging in Publication Data

Davis, Lloyd M
  Contemporary American poetry.

  Includes index.
  1. American poetry--20th century--Bibliography.
I. Irwin, Robert, 1945-   joint author. II. Title.
Z1231.P7D38   [PS323.5]   016.811'5'4   75-19028
ISBN 0-8108-0832-3

PREFACE

This checklist is intended primarily as a guide to American poetry of the 1950's and 60's, what has become known as "contemporary" or "post-modern" poetry, as opposed to the "modern" period of 1890-1945. We have included, however, earlier works by poets born after 1900 who remained productive after 1950. Our cut-off date of December 31, 1973, has allowed us to include many young poets whose futures, although uncertain at this point, appear promising.

Since, with the proliferation of small press publishing in recent years, it would be impossible for any checklist of this nature even to approach comprehensiveness, we have been forced to impose certain limitations. We have eliminated, for example, vanity press books (except for earlier books by now established poets), collaborations, translations (except where combined with original poems), greeting card and other light verse, children's books (except those of well known poets), broadsides, reprints of earlier editions (except where enlargements or revisions are concerned), and books of chiefly illustrative materials.

As it was impossible for us to examine at first hand all of the more than 3400 entries, we apologize in advance for the errors and omissions that a work of this scope must necessarily contain.

Among the many persons who have offered us much valuable assistance, we wish to make grateful acknowledgment to Ruel E. Foster, the English departmental chairman at West Virginia University, whose scholarship has served as an inspiration and whose support in the early days of the project was most encouraging, and to our friend and colleague, S. B. Gribble, Assistant Director of the West Virginia University Libraries, who gave generously of his time, knowledge, and expert advice, and who made available to us the invaluable resources of his reference and technical processes staffs.

Morgantown, W. Va.   L. D.
October 10, 1974   R. I.

THE CHECKLIST

ABISH, Walter
1. Duel site. New York: Tibor de Nagy, 1970.

ACKERSON, Duane
2. Recycle this poem. Pocatello, ID: Dragonfly, 1971.
3. UA flight to Chicago. Crete, NE: Best Cellar, 1971.
4. Weathering. Reno: West Coast Poetry Review, 1973.

ACKLEY, Randall
5. Troll songs. Bowling Green, OH: Tribal, 1971.

ADDISON, Lloyd
6. The aura & the umbra. Detroit: Broadside, 1970.

ADLER, Lucile
7. The traveling out, and other poems. New York: Macmillan, 1967.

AGEE, James
8. Permit me voyage. New Haven: Yale University Press, 1934.
9. The collected poems of James Agee. Boston: Houghton Mifflin, 1968.

AHERN, Tom
10. Transcript. Providence, RI: Burning Deck, 1972.

AI [Florence Anthony]
11. Cruelty. Boston: Houghton Mifflin, 1973.

ALDAN, Daisy
12. Love poems of Daisy Aldan. New York: Barlenmir House, 1972.

ALDRIDGE, Richard
13. An apology both ways. Bloomington: Indiana University Press, 1957.
14. Down through the clouds, the sea. Francestown, NH: Golden Quill, 1963.

ALEXANDER, D.
15. Not a word. Berkeley: Oyez, 1966.

1

16.   Mules balk.   Mattar Publishers, 1969.

ALEXANDER, Floyce
17.   Ravines.   Berkeley: Stone Marrow, 1971.
18.   Machete.   Northwood Narrows, NH: Lillabulero, 1972.

ALEXANDER, James
19.   Eturnature.   Santa Barbara: Open Space, 1965.
20.   The Jack Rabbit poem.   San Francisco: White Rabbit,
       1966.

ALHAMISI, Ahmed (Le Graham)
21.   The black narrator.   Detroit: Black Arts, 1966.
22.   Black spiritual gods.   Detroit: Black Arts, 1968.
23.   Guerrilla warfare.   Detroit: Black Arts, 1970.
24.   Holy ghosts.   Detroit: Broadside, 1972.

ALLEN, Dick
25.   Anon, and various time machine poems.   New York:
       Delacorte, 1971.

ALLEN, Robert
26.   Valhalla at the OK.   Ithaca, NY: Ithaca House, 1971.

ALLEN, Samuel (Paul Vesey)
27.   Ivory tusks.   Millbrook, NY: Kriya, 1968.

ALLEN, Steve
28.   Windfall.   Privately printed, 1946.
29.   Wry on the rocks.   New York: Holt, 1956.

AMES, Bernice
30.   Antelope bread.   Denver: Swallow, 1966.

AMINI, Johari
31.   Let's go some where.   Chicago: Third World, 1970.

AMMONS, A. R.
32.   Ommateum, with doxology.   Philadelphia: Dorrance, 1955.
33.   Expressions of sea level.   Columbus: Ohio State Univer-
       sity Press, 1964.
34.   Corsons Inlet.   Ithaca, NY: Cornell University Press,
       1965.
35.   Tape for the turn of the year.   Ithaca, NY: Cornell Uni-
       versity Press, 1965.
36.   Northfield poems.   Ithaca, NY: Cornell University Press,
       1966.
37.   Selected poems.   Ithaca, NY: Cornell University Press,
       1968.
38.   Uplands.   New York: Norton, 1970.
39.   Briefings; poems small and easy.   New York: Norton,
       1971.
40.   Collected poems, 1951-1971.   New York: Norton, 1972.

3 Anania

ANANIA, Michael
41. The color of dust. Chicago: Swallow, 1970.

ANDERSON, Doug
42. The one real poem is life. New York: Braziller, 1973.

ANDERSON, Jack
43. The hurricane lamp. Trumansburg, NY: New/Books, 1968.
44. The invention of New Jersey. Pittsburgh: University of Pittsburgh Press, 1969.

ANDERSON, Jon
45. Looking for Jonathan. Pittsburgh: University of Pittsburgh Press, 1968.
46. Death & friends. Pittsburgh: University of Pittsburgh Press, 1970.

ANGELOU, Maya
47. Just give me a cool drink of water 'fore I die. New York: Random House, 1971.

ANGOFF, Charles
48. The bell of time. New York: Manyland Books, 1967.
49. Memoranda for tomorrow. New York: Yoseloff, 1968.
50. Prayers at midnight. New York: Manyland Books, 1971.

ANSEN, Alan
51. The old religion. New York: Tibor de Nagy, 1959.
52. Disorderly houses. Middletown, CT: Wesleyan University Press, 1961.
53. Believe and tremble. Athens: privately printed, 1963.
54. Field report. Athens: privately printed, 1963.
55. Day by day. Athens: privately printed, 1966.

ANTIN, David
56. Autobiography. New York: Something Else, 1967.
57. Definitions. New York: Caterpillar, 1967.
58. Code of flag behavior. Los Angeles: Black Sparrow, 1968.
59. Meditations. Los Angeles: Black Sparrow, 1971.
60. Talking. New York: Kulchur, 1972.

ANTONINUS, Brother (William Everson)
61. These are the ravens. San Leandro, CA: Greater West, 1935.
62. The masculine dead. Prairie City, IL: 1939.
63. San Joaquin. Los Angeles: Ward Ritchie, 1939.
64. The Waldport poems. Waldport, OR: 1943.
65. The residual years; poems, 1940-1941. Waldport, OR: Untide, 1944.
66. War elegies. Waldport, OR: Untide, 1944.
67. Poems MCMXLII. Waldport, OR: Untide, 1945.

68. The residual years. New York: New Directions, 1948.
69. A privacy of speech; ten poems in sequence. Berkeley:
       Equinox, 1949.
70. Triptych for the living. Oakland, CA: Seraphim, 1951.
71. The crooked lines of God; poems, 1949-1954. Detroit:
       University of Detroit Press, 1959.
72. The year's declension. Berkeley: Berkeley Albion, 1961.
73. The hazards of holiness; poems, 1957-1960. Garden City,
       NY: Doubleday, 1962.
74. The poet is dead (a memorial for Robinson Jeffers). San
       Francisco: Auerhahn, 1964.
75. The blowing of the seed. New Haven: H. W. Wenning,
       1966.
76. Single source; the early poems of William Everson, 1934-
       1940. Berkeley: Oyez, 1966.
77. In the fictive wish. Berkeley: Oyez, 1967.
78. The rose of solitude. Garden City, NY: Doubleday, 1967.
79. A canticle to the waterbirds. Berkeley: Eizo, 1968.
80. The springing of the blade. Reno: Black Rock, 1968.
81. The city does not die. Berkeley: Oyez, 1969.
82. The last crusade. Berkeley: Oyez, 1969.
83. Who is she that looketh forth as the morning. Berkeley:
       Serendipity, 1970.
84. Earth poetry. Berkeley: Oyez, 1971.

APPLEMAN, Philip
85. Summer love and surf. Nashville: Vanderbilt University
       Press, 1968.

APPLETON, Sarah
86. The plenitude we cry for. Garden City, NY: Doubleday,
       1972.

ARNETT, Carroll
87. Then. New Rochelle, NY: Elizabeth, 1965.
88. Not only that. New Rochelle, NY: Elizabeth, 1967.
89. Like a wall. New Rochelle, NY: Elizabeth, 1969.
90. Through the woods. New Rochelle, NY: Elizabeth, 1971.
91. Earlier. New Rochelle, NY: Elizabeth, 1972.
92. Come. New Rochelle, NY: Elizabeth, 1973.

ASHBERY, John
93. Turandot and other poems. New York: Tibor de Nagy,
       1953.
94. Some trees. New Haven: Yale University Press, 1956;
       New York: Corinth, 1970.
95. Poems. New York: Tiber Press, 1960.
96. The tennis court oath. Middletown, CT: Wesleyan Uni-
       versity Press, 1962.
97. Rivers and mountains. New York: Holt, 1966.
98. Selected poems. London: Jonathan Cape, 1967.
99. Sunrise in suburbia. New York: Phoenix Book Shop, 1968.
100. Fragment. Los Angeles: Black Sparrow Press, 1969.

101.   The double dream of spring. New York: Dutton, 1970.
102.   Three poems. New York: Viking, 1972.

ATKINS, Russell
    103.   Phenomena. Wilberforce, OH: Wilberforce University
          Press, 1961.
    104.   The abortionist and the corpse. Cleveland: Free
          Lance, 1965.
    105.   Heretofore. London: Breman, 1968.
    106.   Maleficum. Cleveland: Free Lance Press, 1971.

ATKINSON, Ron
    107.   Looking for my name. Lenox, MA: Lenox Bookstore
          Press, 1972.

AUBERT, Alvin
    108.   Against the blues. Detroit: Broadside, 1972.

AUDEN, W. H.
    109.   Poems. SHS, 1928.
    110.   Poems. London: Faber, 1930, rev. 1933; New York:
          Random House, 1934.
    111.   The orators: an English study. London: Faber, 1932,
          rev. 1966.
    112.   Look, stranger! London: Faber, 1936; [as] On this
          island, New York: Random House, 1937.
    113.   Spain. London: Faber, 1937.
    114.   Selected poems. London: Faber, 1938.
    115.   Some poems. London: Faber, 1940.
    116.   Another time. New York: Random House, and London:
          Faber, 1940.
    117.   The double man. New York: Random House, 1941; [as]
          New Year letter, London: Faber, 1941.
    118.   For the time being: a Christmas oratorio. New York:
          Random House, 1944; London: Faber, 1945.
    119.   Collected poetry. New York: Random House, 1945.
    120.   The age of anxiety: a baroque eclogue. New York:
          Random House, 1947; London: Faber, 1948.
    121.   Collected shorter poems, 1930-1944. London: Faber, 1950.
    122.   Nones. New York: Random House, and London: Faber,
          1952.
    123.   The shield of Achilles. New York: Random House, and
          London: Faber, 1955.
    124.   The old man's road. New York: Voyages Press, 1956.
    125.   Selected poetry. New York: Modern Library, 1959.
    126.   Homage to Clio. New York: Random House, and Lon-
          don: Faber, 1960.
    127.   About the house. New York: Random House, 1965;
          London: Faber, 1966.
    128.   Collected shorter poems, 1927-1957. London: Faber,
          1966; New York: Random House, 1967.
    129.   Collected longer poems. London: Faber, 1968.
    130.   Selected poems. London: Faber, 1968.

131. City without walls. London: Faber, 1969.
132. Academic graffiti. New York: Random House, 1971.
133. Epistle of a godson, and other poems. New York: Random House, 1972.

AXELROD, David
134. Myths, dreams & dances. Wrentham, MA: Despa, 1972.

BAGG, Robert
135. Madonna of the cello. Middletown, CT: Wesleyan University Press, 1961.
136. Scrawny sonnets. Urbana: University of Illinois Press, 1973.
137. Trompe l'ame. Urbana: University of Illinois Press, 1973.

BAKER, Carlos
138. A year and a day. Nashville: Vanderbilt University Press, 1963.

BAKER, Howard
139. A letter from the country. Norfolk, CT: New Directions, 1941.
140. Ode to the sea, and other poems. Denver: Swallow, 1966.

BANKS, Russell
141. Waiting to freeze. Northwood Narrows, NH: Lillabulero, 1969.

BANY, Amalia M.
142. Dear Richard. Denver: Swallow, 1965.

BARAKA, Imamu Amiri see JONES, LeRoi

BARKER, Eric
143. The planetary heart. Mill Valley, CA: Wings, 1942.
144. Directions in the sun. New York: Gotham Book Mart, 1956.
145. In easy dark. Los Angeles: H. & R. Hanson, 1958.
146. A ring of willows. New York: New Directions, 1961.
147. Looking for water; new and selected poems. New York: October House, 1964.

BARKS, Coleman
148. The juice. New York: Harper & Row, 1971.

BARNARD, Mary
149. A few poems. Portland, OR: Reed College, 1952.

BARNES, Keith
    150. Born to flying glass. New York: Harcourt, Brace,
        1967.

BARNSTONE, Aliki
    151. The real tin flower; poems about the world at nine.
        New York: Crowell-Collier, 1968.

BARO, Gene
    152. Northwind and other poems. New York: Scribner, 1959.
    153. A view of water. Newcastle-on-Tyne: Northern House,
        1965.

BARRAX, Gerald W.
    154. Another kind of rain. Pittsburgh: University of Pitts-
        burgh Press, 1970.

BARTLETT, Elizabeth
    155. Poetry concerto. Flushing, NY: Sparrow Magazine
        Press, 1961.
    156. It takes practice not to die. Santa Barbara: Van Riper
        & Thompson, 1966.
    157. Threads. New York: Unicorn, 1968.

BATES, Scott
    158. Poems of war resistance. New York: Grossman, 1969.

BAXTER, Charles
    159. Chameleon. New York: New Rivers, 1970.

BAYES, Ron
    160. Dust and desire. Denver: Big Mountain, 1960.
    161. Cages and journeys. Elms Court: A. H. Stockwell,
        1964.
    162. Child outside my window. Bear Press, 1965.
    163. Turtle three. Sacramento: GRR Books, 1966.
    164. Ejection. Homestead, FL: Olivant, 1967.
    165. X-ing warm. Prensa de Lagar, 1968.
    166. History of the turtle, books I-IV. Homestead, FL:
        Olivant, 1970.
    167. Porpoise. Union, OR: Ramah, 1971.
    168. The casketmaker; selected shorter poems, 1960-1970.
        Winston-Salem, NC: J. F. Blair, 1972.

BEAGLE, Peter
    169. The California feeling. Garden City, NY: Doubleday,
        1969.

BEAN, Stephen
    170. The five-year-old voyage. Bellingham, WA: Goliards,
        1970.

BELITT, Ben
    171. The five-fold mesh. New York: Knopf, 1938.
    172. Wilderness stair. New York: Grove, 1955.
    173. The enemy joy, new and selected poems. Chicago:
          University of Chicago Press, 1964.
    174. Nowhere but light; poems, 1964-1969. Chicago: Univer-
          sity of Chicago Press, 1970.

BELL, Charles G.
    175. Songs for a new America. Bloomington: Indiana Univer-
          sity Press, 1953.
    176. Delta return. Bloomington: Indiana University Press,
          1956.

BELL, Marvin
    177. Poems for Nathan and Saul. Mount Vernon, IA: Hill-
          side Press, 1966.
    178. Things we dreamt we died for. Iowa City: Stone Wall,
          1966.
    179. A probable volume of dreams. New York: Atheneum,
          1969.
    180. The escape into you; a sequence. New York: Atheneum,
          1971.
    181. Woo havoc. Somerville, MA: Barn Dream, 1971.

BELLAMANN, Katherine
    182. Two sides of a poem. Denver: Swallow, 1955.

BENEDIKT, Michael
    183. Changes: 21 poems. Detroit: New Fresco, 1961.
    184. 8 poems. New York: 1966.
    185. The body. Middletown, CT: Wesleyan University Press,
          1968.
    186. Sky. Middletown, CT: Wesleyan University Press, 1970.
    187. Mole notes. Middletown, CT: Wesleyan University
          Press, 1971.

BENTLEY, Beth
    188. Phone calls from the dead. Athens: Ohio University
          Press, 1970.

BENTLEY, Nelson
    189. Sea lion caves, and other poems. Denver: Swallow,
          1966.

BERG, Stephen
    190. Bearing weapons. Iowa City: Cummington, 1963.
    191. The queen's triangle; a romance. West Branch, IA:
          Cummington, 1970.
    192. The daughters. Indianapolis: Bobbs-Merrill, 1971.

BERGÉ, Carol
    193. The vulnerable island. Cleveland: Renegade, 1964.

194. Lumina. Cleveland: Renegade, 1965.
195. Circles, as in the eye. New Mexico: Desert Review, 1968.
196. Poems made of skin. Toronto: Weed/Flower, 1968.
197. An American romance; the Alan poems, a journal. Los Angeles: Black Sparrow, 1969.
198. The chambers. Aylesford Priory, Kent: Aylesford Review, 1969.
199. From a soft angle: poems about women. Indianapolis: Bobbs-Merrill, 1971.

BERKSON, Bill
200. Saturday Night: poems, 1960-1961. New York: Tibor de Nagy, 1961.
201. Shining leaves. New York: Angel Hair, 1969.
202. Recent visitors. New York: Angel Hair, 1973.

BERNSTEIN, Leonard S.
203. The black snowman & other poems. London, New York: Abelard-Schuman, 1971.

BERRIGAN, Daniel
204. Time without number. New York: Macmillan, 1957.
205. Encounters. Cleveland: World, 1960.
206. The world for wedding ring. New York: Macmillan, 1962.
207. No one walks waters. New York: Macmillan, 1966.
208. Consequences: truth and 1967. New York: Macmillan, 1968.
209. Love, love at the end. New York: Macmillan, 1968.
210. Night flight to Hanoi. New York: Macmillan, 1968.
211. False gods, real men. New York: Macmillan, 1969.
212. Crime trial. Boston: Impressions Workshop, 1970.
213. America is hard to find. Garden City, NY: Doubleday, 1972.
214. Prison poems. Greensboro, NC: Unicorn, 1973.
215. Selected and new poems. Garden City, NY: Doubleday, 1973.

BERRIGAN, Ted
216. The sonnets. New York: Grove, 1967.
217. Many happy returns. New York: Corinth, 1969.
218. In the early morning rain. New York: Cape Goliard, 1971.

BERRY, D. C.
219. Saigon cemetery. Athens: University of Georgia Press, 1972.

BERRY, Wendell
220. The broken ground. New York: Harcourt, Brace, 1964.
221. November twenty-six, nineteen hundred sixty-three, poem. New York: Braziller, 1964.

222. Openings. New York: Harcourt, Brace, 1968.
223. Findings. Iowa City: Prairie, 1969.
224. Farming: a hand book. New York: Harcourt, Brace, 1970.
225. The country of marriage. New York: Harcourt, Brace, 1973.

BERRYMAN, John
226. Poems. Norfolk, CT: New Directions, 1942.
227. The dispossessed. New York: Sloane, 1948.
228. Homage to Mistress Bradstreet. New York: Farrar, Straus, 1956.
229. His thought made pockets & the plane buckt. Pawlet, VT: Fredericks, 1958.
230. 77 dream songs. New York: Farrar, Straus, 1964.
231. Berryman's sonnets. New York: Farrar, Straus, 1967; London: Faber, 1968.
232. Short poems. New York: Farrar, Straus, 1967.
233. His toy, his dream, his rest; 308 dream songs. New York: Farrar, Straus, 1968; London: Faber, 1969.
234. The dream songs. New York: Farrar, Straus, 1969.
235. Love & fame. New York: Farrar, Straus, 1970.
236. Delusions, etc. New York: Farrar, Straus, 1972.
237. Selected poems, 1938-1968. London: Faber, 1972.

BERTOLINO, James
238. Day of change. Milwaukee: Gunrunner, 1968.
239. Drool. Madison, WI: Quixote, 1968.
240. Ceremony. Milwaukee: Morgan, 1969.
241. Maize. Madison, WI: Abraxas, 1969.
242. Mr. Nobody. Menomonie, WI: Ox Head, 1969.
243. Stone-marrow. Madison, WI: Anachoreta/Abraxas, 1969.
244. Becoming human. Albuquerque, NM: Road Runner, 1970.
245. Edging through. Ithaca, NY: Stone-Marrow, 1972.
246. Employed. Ithaca, NY: Ithaca House, 1972.

BERTOLINO, Lois
247. Garden of Eve. Madison, WI: Abraxas, 1968.

BIALY, Harvey
248. Love's will. Annandale-on-Hudson, NY: Matter Books, 1968.
249. The Geronimo poem. Gambier, OH: Pothanger, 1969.
250. Babalon 156. Berkeley: Sand Dollar, 1970.
251. Susanna Martin. San Francisco: Dave Haselwood, 1970.

BIGGER, Duff
252. Soleares. Madison, WI: Abraxas, 1970.

BIRCH, McLane
253. The kandi man. Detroit: Broadside, 1970.

BIRNBAUM, Henry
    254. Limits and trials. New York: New York University
        Press, 1970.

BISHOP, Elizabeth
    255. North & south. Boston: Houghton Mifflin, 1946.
    256. Poems. London: Chatto and Windus, 1955.
    257. Poems: North & South. A cold spring. Boston:
        Houghton Mifflin, 1955.
    258. Questions of travel. New York: Farrar, Straus, 1965.
    259. Selected poems. London: Chatto and Windus, 1967.
    260. The ballad of the burglar of Babylon. New York: Far-
        rar, Straus, 1968.
    261. The complete poems. New York: Farrar, Straus, 1969.

BLACK, Charles Lund
    262. Telescope & islands. Denver: Swallow, 1963.

BLACKBURN, Paul
    263. The dissolving fabric. Majorca: Divers, 1955; Toronto:
        Mother Island, 1966.
    264. Brooklyn-Manhattan transit. New York: Totem, 1960.
    265. The nets. New York: Trobar, 1961.
    266. Sing-song. New York: Caterpillar, 1966.
    267. The Reardon poems. Madison, WI: Perishable, 1967.
    268. The cities. New York: Grove, 1967.
    269. In. on. or about the premises. London: Cape Goliard,
        1968.
    270. Early selected y mas: collected poems, 1949-1961.
        Los Angeles: Black Sparrow, 1972.

BLAKE, Howard
    271. The island self. Boston: Godine, 1973.

BLASER, Robin
    272. The moth poem. San Francisco: Open Space, 1964.
    273. Cups. San Francisco: Four Seasons, 1968.

BLAZEK, Douglas
    274. All gods must learn to kill. Demarest, NJ: Analecta,
        1968.
    275. Sting & die. Eugene, OR: Toad, 1968.
    276. Fuck off, unless you take-off that mask. Milwaukee:
        Gunrunner, 1969.
    277. I advance with loaded rose. San Francisco: Twowindows,
        1969.
    278. Life in a common gun. Madison, WI: Quixote, 1969.
    279. Baptismal corruption in the sunflower patch. Sacramen-
        to, CA: Runcible Spoon, 1970.
    280. Climbing blind. Cardiff: Second Aeon, 1970.
    281. Flux and reflux; journies in a magical fluid. Berkeley:
        Oyez, 1970.
    282. Skull juices. San Francisco: Twowindows, 1970.

BLY, Robert
  283. Silence in the snowy fields. Middletown, CT: Wesleyan University Press, 1962.
  284. The light around the body. New York: Harper & Row, 1967.
  285. The morning glory. San Francisco: Kayak, 1969.
  286. The shadow-mothers. New York: Harper & Row, 1970.
  287. The teeth-mother naked at last. San Francisco: City Lights, 1970.
  288. Jumping out of bed. Barre, MA: Barre Publishers, 1972.
  289. Sleepers joining hands. New York: Harper & Row, 1972.
  290. Point Reyes poems. San Francisco: Mudra, 1973.

BOAR, Gerard (see also BORREGAARD, Ebbe)
  291. Sketches for 13 sonnets. Berkeley: Oyez, 1969.

BOCKRIS, Victor
  292. In America. Norwood, PA: Telegraph Books, 1973.

BODE, Carl
  293. The sacred seasons. Denver: Swallow, 1953.
  294. The calendar of love, sonnets. Swinford: Fantasy, 1959.
  295. The man behind you. New York: Dutton, 1960; London: Heineman, 1959.

BOER, Charles
  296. The odes. Chicago: Swallow, 1969.
  297. Varmint Q: an epic poem on the life of William Clarke Quantrill. Chicago: Swallow, 1972.

BOGARDUS, Edgar
  298. Various jangling keys. New Haven: Yale University Press, 1953.
  299. Last poems. Gambier, OH: Kenyon Review Press, 1960.

BOND, Harold
  300. The northern wall. Boston: Northeastern University Press, 1969.
  301. Dancing on water. Iowa City: Cummington, 1970.

BONNETTE, Jeanne DeLamarter
  302. In this place. Fort Smith, AR: South and West, 1971.

BOOTH, Philip
  303. Letter from a distant land. New York: Viking, 1957.
  304. The islanders. New York: Viking, 1961.
  305. Weathers and edges. New York: Viking, 1966.
  306. Margins. New York: Viking, 1970.

BOOTMAN, Tyler
   307. Myself in the street. New York: October House, 1966.

BORREGAARD, Ebbe (see also BOAR, Gerard)
   308. The Wapitis. San Francisco: White Rabbit, 1960.

BOURLAND, George
   309. Refugees from nowhere. San Francisco: Twowindows,
        1968.

BOWERS, Edgar
   310. The form of loss. Denver: Swallow, 1956.
   311. The astronomers. Denver: Swallow, 1965.
   312. Living together: new and selected poems. Boston:
        Godine, 1973.

BOWLES, Paul
   313. Scenes by Paul Bowles. Los Angeles: Black Sparrow,
        1968.
   314. The thicket of spring; poems, 1926-1969. Los Angeles:
        Black Sparrow, 1972.

BOWYER, John Wilson
   315. The celebrated Mrs. Centlivre. Durham, NC: Duke
        University Press, 1952.

BOXER, Ray
   316. Along the edges. New York: The Smith, 1971.

BOYLE, Kay
   317. A glad day. Norfolk, CT: New Directions, 1938.
   318. American citizen. New York: Simon and Schuster,
        1944.
   319. Collected poems. New York: Knopf, 1962.
   320. The long walk at San Francisco State. New York:
        Grove, 1970.
   321. Testament for my students and other poems. Garden
        City, NY: Doubleday, 1970.

BOZE, Arthur
   322. Black words. Detroit: Broadside, 1972.

BRAINARD, Franklin
   323. Rain gatherer. Madison, MN: The Seventies, 1972.

BRAINARD, Joe
   324. I remember. New York: Angel Hair, 1970.
   325. New work. Los Angeles: Black Sparrow, 1973.

BRANDI, John
   326. Poem afternoon in a square of Guadalajara. Maya
        Quarto Six, 1969.
   327. One week of mornings at Dry Creek. Santa Barbara, 1971.

BRAUN, Henry
    328. The Vergil woods. New York: Atheneum, 1968.

BRAUN, Richard
    329. Companions to your doom. Detroit: New Fresco, 1961.
    330. Children passing. Austin: University of Texas Press, 1962.
    331. The foreclosure. Urbana: University of Illinois Press, 1972.

BRAUTIGAN, Richard
    332. The return of the rivers. San Francisco: Inferno, 1957.
    333. The Galilee hitch-hiker. San Francisco: White Rabbit, 1958.
    334. Lay the marble tea, twenty-four poems. San Francisco: Carp, 1959.
    335. The octopus frontier. San Francisco: Carp, 1960.
    336. The pill versus the Springhill mine disaster. San Francisco: Four Seasons, 1968.
    337. Rommel drives on deep into Egypt. New York: Delacorte, 1970.

BREMSER, Ray
    338. Poems of madness. New York: Paper Book Gallery, 1965.
    339. Angel; the work of one night in the dark, solitary confinement, New Jersey State Prison, Trenton. New York: Tompkins Square, 1967.
    340. Drive suite; an essay on composition, materials, references, etc. San Francisco: Nova Broadcast, 1968.

BRIGHAM, Besmilr.
    341. Heaved from the earth. New York: Knopf, 1971.

BRILLIANT, Alan
    342. At trial. Santa Barbara: Unicorn, 1969.
    343. Searching for signs. Santa Barbara: Unicorn, 1969.
    344. Journeyman. Greensboro, NC: Unicorn, 1971.

BRINNIN, John Malcolm
    345. The garden is political. New York: Macmillan, 1942.
    346. The Lincoln lyrics. New York: New Directions, 1942.
    347. No arch, no triumph. New York: Knopf, 1945.
    348. Selected poems. Boston: Little, Brown, 1963.
    349. Skin diving in the Virgins, and other poems. New York: Delacorte, 1970.
    350. The sorrows of cold stone; poems, 1940-1950. Westport, CT: Greenwood, 1971.

BROCK, Edwin
    351. The portraits & the poses. New York: New Directions, 1973.

BRODEY, James
  352.   Fleeing madly south.   New York: Clothesline Editions,
             1967.
  353.   Identikit.   New York: Angel Hair, 1967.
  354.   Long distance quote.   Los Angeles: Mustard Seed, 1968.

BROMIGE, David
  355.   The gathering.   Buffalo, NY: Sumbooks, 1965.
  356.   The ends of the earth.   Los Angeles: Black Sparrow,
             1968.
  357.   Please, like me.   Los Angeles: Black Sparrow, 1968.
  358.   Threads.   Los Angeles: Black Sparrow, 1971.

BRONK, William
  359.   The world, the worldless.   New York: New Directions,
             1964.
  360.   The empty hands.   New Rochelle, NY: Elizabeth, 1969.
  361.   That tantalus.   New Rochelle, NY: Elizabeth, 1971.
  362.   To praise the music.   New Rochelle, NY: Elizabeth,
             1972.
  363.   Utterances.   Providence, RI: Burning Deck, 1972.

BROOKHOUSE, Christopher
  364.   Scattered light.   Chapel Hill: University of North Caro-
             lina Press, 1969.

BROOKS, Gwendolyn
  365.   A street in Bronzeville.   New York: Harper, 1945.
  366.   Annie Allen.   New York: Harper, 1949.
  367.   Bronzeville boys and girls.   New York: Harper, 1956.
  368.   The bean eaters.   New York: Harper, 1960.
  369.   Selected poems.   New York: Harper & Row, 1963.
  370.   For Illinois, 1968; a sesquicentennial poem.   Chicago,
             1968.
  371.   In the Mecca.   New York: Harper & Row, 1968.
  372.   Riot.   Detroit: Broadside, 1969.
  373.   Family pictures.   Detroit: Broadside, 1970.
  374.   Aloneness.   Detroit: Broadside, 1971.
  375.   Black steel.   Detroit: Broadside, 1971.
  376.   Jump bad.   Detroit: Broadside, 1971.
  377.   The world of Gwendolyn Brooks.   New York: Harper &
             Row, 1971.
  378.   Report from part one.   Detroit: Broadside, 1972.

BROSMAN, Catherine Savage
  379.   Watering.   Athens: University of Georgia Press, 1972.

BROUGHTON, James
  380.   Songs for certain children.   San Francisco: Adrian
             Wilson, 1947.
  381.   The playground.   San Francisco: Centaur, 1949.
  382.   The ballad of mad Jenny.   San Francisco, 1950.
  383.   An almanac for amorists.   New York: Grove, 1955.

384. True & false unicorn. New York: Grove, 1957.
385. The right playmate. San Francisco: Pterodactyl Press,
       1964.
386. Tidings, poems at the land's edge. San Francisco:
       Pearce & Bennett, 1965.
387. The water circle. San Francisco: Pterodactyl Press,
       1965.
388. High kukus. New York: Jargon, 1968.
389. Look in look out. Eugene, OR: Toad, 1968.
390. All about it. Eugene, OR: Toad, 1969.
391. Whistling in the labyrinth. Penland, NC: Jargon, 1969.

BROWN, Rita Mae
392. The hand that cradles the rock. New York: New York
       University Press, 1971.

BROWN, Rosalie
393. The grasshopper's man, and other poems. New Haven:
       Yale University Press, 1949.

BROWN, Rosellen
394. Some deaths in the delta, and other poems. Amherst:
       University of Massachusetts Press, 1970.

BROWNSTEIN, Michael
395. Behind the wheel. New York: "C" Press, 1967.
396. Highway to the sky. New York: Columbia University
       Press, 1969.
397. American tantrums. New York: Angel Hair, 1973.

BRUCE, Lennart
398. Making the rounds. San Francisco: Kayak, 1967.
399. The mullioned window. San Francisco: Kayak, 1970.
400. Letter of credit. Santa Cruz, CA: Kayak, 1972.

BRUCHAC, Joseph
401. First deer and other poems. Ithaca, NY: Ithaca House,
       1971.
402. Indian mountain. Ithaca, NY: Ithaca House, 1971.
403. The buffalo in the Syracuse zoo. Greenfield Center,
       NY: The Greenfield Review Press, 1973.

BRUGNOLA, Orlanda
404. King of thornbushes. Berkeley: Oyez, 1972.

BUCKNER, John
405. It might be a window. Sacramento, CA: Runcible
       Spoon, 1968.

BUELL, Frederick
406. Theseus and other poems. Ithaca, NY: Ithaca House,
       1971.

BUKOWSKI, Charles
407. Flower, fist and bestial wall. Eureka, CA: Hearse, 1959.
408. Longshot poems for broke players. New York: 7 Poets, 1961.
409. Run with the hunted. Chicago: Midwest Poetry Chapbooks, 1962.
410. It catches my heart in its hands. New Orleans: Loujon, 1963.
411. Cold dogs in the courtyard. Chicago: Chicago Literary Times, 1965.
412. Confessions of a man insane enough to live with beasts. San Francisco: Mimeo Press, 1965.
413. Crucifix in a deathhand: new poems, 1963-1965. New York: L. Stuart, 1965.
414. The curtains are waving, and people walk through the afternoon here and in Berlin and in New York City and in Mexico. San Francisco: Black Sparrow, 1967.
415. At terror street and agony way. Los Angeles: Black Sparrow, 1968.
416. Poems written before jumping out of an 8-story window. Berkeley: Litmus, 1968.
417. The days run away like wild horses. Los Angeles: Black Sparrow, 1970.
418. Post office. Los Angeles: Black Sparrow, 1971.
419. Mockingbird wish me luck. Los Angeles: Black Sparrow, 1972.

BULLIS, Jerald
420. Taking up the serpent. Ithaca, NY: Ithaca House, 1973.

BURDEN, Jean
421. Naked as the glass. New York: October House, 1963.

BURFORD, William
422. Man now. Dallas: Southern Methodist University Press, 1954.
423. Faccia della terra (English and Italian). Bologna: Libreria Palmaverde, 1960.
424. A world. Austin: University of Texas Press, 1962.
425. A beginning. New York: Norton, 1966.

BURKARD, Michel
426. None river. Boston: Barn Dream, 1973.

BURNSHAW, Stanley
427. The wheel age. Privately printed, 1928.
428. The iron land. Philadelphia: Centaur, 1936.
429. Early and late testament. New York: Dial, 1952.
430. Caged in an animal's mind. New York: Holt, Rinehart and Winston, 1963.
431. In the terrified radiance. New York: Braziller, 1972.

BURR, Gray
432. A choice of attitudes. Middletown, CT: Wesleyan University Press, 1969.

BURROWS, E. G.
433. The Arctic tern. New York: Grove, 1957.
434. Man fishing. Fremont, MI: Sumac, 1969.

BURT, Nathaniel
435. Rooms in a house. New York: Scribner, 1947.
436. Question on a kite. New York: Scribner, 1950.

BUTCHER, Grace
437. The bright-colored dark. Seven Flowers Press, 1966.
438. More stars than room for. Hiram, OH: Hiram College Press, 1966.
439. Rumors of ecstasy ... rumors of death. Ashland, OH: Ashland Poetry Press, 1971.

CALLOW, Philip
440. The bare wires. Middletown, CT: Wesleyan University Press, 1973.

CAMP, James
441. An edict from the emperor. Providence, RI: Burning Deck, 1968.

CANNON, C. E.
442. Saint Nigger. Detroit: Broadside, 1972.

CANZONERI, Robert
443. Watch us pass. Columbus: Ohio State University Press, 1968.

CARDONA-HINE, Alvaro
444. Romance de Agapito cascante. Costa Rica: Reportorio Americano, 1955.
445. The gathering wave; forty-eight haiku with drawings. Denver: Swallow, 1961.
446. The flesh of utopia. Denver: Swallow, 1966.

CARLILE, Henry
447. The rough-hewn table. Columbia, MO: University of Missouri Press, 1971.

CARRIER, Constance
448. The middle voice. Denver: Swallow, 1954.

CARRIER, Warren
449. The cost of love. Elmhurst, IL: privately printed, 1953.

450.   Toward Montebello. New York: Harper & Row, 1966.

CARRIGAN, Andrew
451.   "3." Fremont, MI: Sumac, 1972.

CARRINGTON, Harold
452.   Drive suite. Detroit: Broadside, 1970.

CARROLL, Jim
453.   4 ups & 1 down. New York: Angel Hair, 1970.
454.   Living at the movies. New York: Goliard/Grossman, 1973.

CARROLL, Paul
455.   Odes. Chicago: Big Table, 1969.
456.   The Luke poems. Chicago: Big Table, 1971.

CARRUTH, Hayden
457.   The crow and the heart, 1946-1959. New York: Macmillan, 1959.
458.   Journey to a known place. Norfolk, CT: New Directions, 1961.
459.   The Norfolk poems, 1 June to 1 September, 1961. Iowa City: Prairie, 1962.
460.   North winter. Iowa City: Prairie, 1964.
461.   Nothing for tigers; poems, 1959-1964. New York: Macmillan, 1965.
462.   Contra mortem. Johnson, VT: Crow's Mark, 1967.
463.   The clay hill anthology. Iowa City: Prairie, 1970.
464.   For you. New York: New Directions, 1970; London: Chatto and Windus, 1971.
465.   Dark world. Santa Cruz, CA: Kayak, 1973.
466.   From snow and rock, from chaos. New York: New Directions, 1973.

CARTER, John Stewart
467.   Poems: an handful with quietness. Boston: Houghton Mifflin, 1966.

CARVER, Raymond
468.   Winter insomnia. Santa Cruz, CA: Kayak, 1970.

CASEY, Bernie
469.   Look at the people. Garden City, NY: Doubleday, 1969.

CASEY, Michael
470.   Obscenities. New Haven: Yale University Press, 1972.

471.   [no entry]

CASSIN, Maxine
472.   A touch of recognition. Denver: Swallow, 1962.

CASSITY, Turner
    473. Watchboy, what of the night? Middletown, CT: Wesleyan University Press, 1966.
    474. Silver out of Shanghai. Atlanta: Planet Mongo, 1973.
    475. Steeplejacks in Babel. Brookline, MA: Godine, 1973.

CAUBLE, Don
    476. Inside out. Portland, OR: privately printed, 1968.
    477. Three on fire. Portland, OR: Dead Angel, 1971.

CERAVOLO, Joseph
    478. Fits of dawn. New York: "C" Press, 1965.
    479. Wild flowers out of gas. New York: Tibor de Nagy, 1967.
    480. Spring in this world of poor mutts. New York: Columbia University Press, 1968.

CHAMBERS, George
    481. The bonnyclabber. Western Springs, IL: December Press, 1972.

CHAPPELL, Fred
    482. The world between the eyes. Baton Rouge: Louisiana State University Press, 1971.

CHARTERS, Samuel
    483. Days, or days as thoughts in a season's uncertainties. Berkeley: Oyez, 1967.
    484. To this place. Berkeley: Oyez, 1969.
    485. From a Swedish notebook. Berkeley: Oyez, 1973.

CHASIN, Helen
    486. Coming close, and other poems. New Haven: Yale University Press, 1968.

CHATFIELD, Hale (Henry Dumas)
    487. Teeth. Trumansburg, NY: Crossing Press, 1967.
    488. At home. Ashland, OH: Ashland Poetry Press, 1971.

CHESTER, Laura
    489. The all night salt licks. Bowling Green, OH: Tribal, 1972.

CHIGOUNIS, Evans
    490. Secret lives. Middletown, CT: Wesleyan University Press, 1972.

CHISHOLM, Hugh
    491. Atlantic City cantata. New York: Farrar, Straus, 1951.

CIARDI, John
    492. Homeward to America. New York: Holt, 1940.
    493. Other skies. Boston: Little, Brown, 1947.

494. Live another day. New York: Twayne, 1949.
495. From time to time. New York: Twayne, 1951.
496. As if; poems new and selected. New Brunswick, NJ: Rutgers University Press, 1955.
497. I marry you; a sheaf of love poems. New Brunswick, NJ: Rutgers University Press, 1958.
498. 39 poems. New Brunswick, NJ: Rutgers University Press, 1959.
499. I met a man. Boston: Houghton Mifflin, 1961.
500. In the stoneworks. New Brunswick, NJ: Rutgers University Press, 1961.
501. The man who sang the sillies. Philadelphia: Lippincott, 1961.
502. In fact. New Brunswick, NJ: Rutgers University Press, 1962.
503. You read to me, I'll read to you. Philadelphia: Lippincott, 1962.
504. Person to person. New Brunswick, NJ: Rutgers University Press, 1964.
505. This strangest everything. New Brunswick, NJ: Rutgers University Press, 1966.
506. An alphabestiary. Philadelphia: Lippincott, 1967.
507. A genesis; 15 poems by John Ciardi. New York: Touchstone, 1967.
508. Someone could win a polar bear. Philadelphia: Lippincott, 1970.
509. Lives of X. New Brunswick, NJ: Rutgers University Press, 1971.

CLAREMON, Neil
510. East by southwest. New York: Simon and Schuster, 1970.
511. West of the American dream; poems to be read aloud. New York: Morrow, 1973.

CLARK, L. D.
512. Dark night of the body. Austin: University of Texas Press, 1964.

CLARK, Thomas A.
513. Some particulars. Millerton, NY: Jargon, 1973.

CLARK, Tom
514. Airplanes. Brightlingsea, Essex: Once Press, 1966.
515. The sand burg. London: Ferry Press, 1966.
516. Sonnet. New York: Angel Hair, 1968.
517. Stones. New York: Harper & Row, 1968.
518. Emperor of the animals. London: Goliard, c. 1969.
519. Air. New York: Harper & Row, 1970.
520. Neil Young. New York: Angel Hair, 1970.
521. Green. Los Angeles: Black Sparrow, 1971.
522. John's heart. New York: Goliard/Santa Fe, 1972.
523. Smack. Los Angeles: Black Sparrow, 1972.

CLAUDEL, Alice Moser
    524. Southern season. Pikeville, KY: Pikeville College
          Press, 1972.

CLIFTON, Lucille
    525. Good time. New York: Random House, 1969.
    526. The black BC's. New York: Dutton, 1970.
    527. Good news about the earth. New York: Random House,
          1972.

COBB, Charlie
    528. In the furrows of the world. Tougaloo, MS: Flute Pub-
          lications, 1967.
    529. Everywhere is yours. Chicago: Third World, 1971.

CODRESCU, Andrei
    530. License to carry a gun. Chicago: Big Table, 1970.
    531. & grammar & money. Berkeley: Arif, 1973.
    532. The history of the growth of heaven. New York:
          Braziller, 1973.

COLEMAN, Elliott
    533. The poems of Elliott Coleman. New York: Dutton,
          1936.
    534. An American in Augustland. Chapel Hill: University of
          North Carolina Press, 1940.
    535. Pearl Harbor. Privately printed, 1942.
    536. 27 night sonnets. New York and Milan: New Directions,
          1949.
    537. A glass darkly. Baltimore: Contemporary Poetry, 1952.
    538. 33 night sonnets. Baltimore: Contemporary Poetry,
          1955.
    539. Sonnetti (English and Italian). Bologna: Libreria Anti-
          quaria Palmaverde, 1959.
    540. Mockingbirds at Fort McHenry. Pamplona: Atlantis
          Editions, 1963.
    541. Broken death. Baltimore: Linden Press, 1964.
    542. Rose demonics: 1936-1966. Baltimore: Linden Press,
          1967.

COMBS, Tram
    543. Pilgrim's terrace; poems, American, West Indian. San
          Germán, PR: Editorial La Nueva Salamanca, 1957.
    544. Ceremonies in mind: artists, boys, cats, lovers,
          judges, priests. St. Thomas, VI, 1959.
    545. Saint-Thomas. Middletown, CT: Wesleyan University
          Press, 1965.
    546. Briefs. Franklin, NH: Hillside Press, 1966.

    547-8. [no entry]

CONTOSKI, Victor
    549. Astronomers, jadonnas, and prophecies. La Crosse,

WI: Juniper, 1972.
550. Broken treaties. New York: New Rivers, 1973.

COOK, Albert
551. The Charges. Chicago: Swallow, 1970.

COOLIDGE, Clark
552. Flag flutter and U.S. electric. New York: Lines
 .   Books, 1966.
553. Clark Coolidge. Cambridge, MA: Lines Books, 1967.
554. Ing. New York: Angel Hair, 1969.
555. Space. New York: Harper & Row, 1970.
556. The so. New York: Adventures in Poetry, 1971.

COOPER, Jane
557. The weather of six mornings. New York: Macmillan,
      1968.

COOPERMAN, Stanley
558. The day of the parrot, and other poems. Lincoln:
      University of Nebraska Press, 1968.
559. The owl behind the door. Toronto: McClelland and
      Stewart, 1968.
560. Cappelbaum's dance. Lincoln: University of Nebraska
      Press, 1970.
561. Cannibals. Ottawa: Oberon, 1972.

CORBETT, William
562. Sunset. Boston: Barn Dream, 1970.

CORMAN, Cid
563. subluna (juvenilia). Boston: privately printed, 1945.
564. Thanksgiving eclogue. New York: Sparrow, 1954.
565. The precisions. New York: Sparrow, 1955.
566. The responses. Bari, Italy: Origin, 1956.
567. The marches. Florence: Origin, 1957.
568. Stances and distances. Matera, Italy: Origin, 1957.
569. A table in provenance. Kyoto: Origin, 1958.
570. Cool gong. Kyoto: Origin, 1958.
571. Cool melon. Kyoto: Origin, 1958.
572. Clocked stone. Kyoto: Origin, 1959.
573. The descent from Daimonji. Kyoto: Origin, 1959.
574. For sure. Kyoto: Origin, 1959.
575. For instance. Kyoto: Origin, 1960.
576. For good. Kyoto: Origin, 1961.
577. Sun rock man. Kyoto: Origin, 1962.
578. In good time. Kyoto: Origin, 1964.
579. In no time. Kyoto: privately printed, 1964.
580. Selected frogs. Kyoto: Origin, 1964.
581. All in all. Kyoto: Origin, 1965.
582. Nonce. New Rochelle, NY: Elizabeth, 1965.
583. For you. Kyoto: Origin, 1966.
584. For granted. New Rochelle, NY: Elizabeth, 1966.

585. Stead. New Rochelle, NY: Elizabeth, 1966.
586. Back roads to far town. Tokyo: Mushinsha, 1967.
587. Words for each other. London: Rapp & Carroll, 1967.
588. & without end. New Rochelle, NY: Elizabeth, 1968.
589. Frogs and others. Tokyo: Mushinsha, 1968.
590. Hearth. Kyoto: Origin, 1968.
591. No less. New Rochelle, NY: Elizabeth, 1968.
592. Nigh. New York: Pierrepont Press, 1969.
593. No more. New Rochelle, NY: Elizabeth, 1969.
594. Plight. New Rochelle, NY: Elizabeth, 1969.
595. Livingdying. New York: New Directions, 1970.
596. Sun rock man. New York: New Directions, 1970.
597. Be quest. New Rochelle, NY: Elizabeth, 1972.
598. Out & out. New Rochelle, NY: Elizabeth, 1972.
599. So far. New Rochelle, NY: Elizabeth, 1973.

CORNISH, Sam
600. In this corner. Baltimore: Fleming McCallister, 1961.
601. People under the window. Baltimore: Sacco, 1962.
602. Generations. Baltimore: Beanbag, 1964.
603. Angles. Baltimore: Beanbag, 1965.
604. Winters. Cambridge, MA: San Souci, 1968.
605. Your hand in mine. New York: Harcourt, Brace, 1970.
606. Generations. Boston: Beacon, 1971.
607. Streets. Chicago: Third World, 1973.

CORRINGTON, John William
608. Where we are. Washington: Charioteer, 1962.
609. The anatomy of love & other poems. Fort Lauderdale: Roman Books, 1964.
610. Mr. Clean and other poems. San Francisco: Amber House, 1964.
611. Lines to the South, and other poems. Baton Rouge: Louisiana State University Press, 1965.

CORSO, Gregory
612. The vestal lady on brattle. Cambridge, MA: Richard Brukenfeld, 1955.
613. Bomb. San Francisco: City Lights, 1958.
614. Gasoline. San Francisco: City Lights, 1958.
615. The happy birthday of death. New York: J. Laughlin, 1960.
616. Long live man. Norfolk, CT: New Directions, 1962.
617. Selected poems. London: Eyre and Spottiswoode, 1962.
618. The mutation of the spirit. New York: Death Press, 1964.
619. There is yet time to run back through life and expiate all that's been sadly done. 1965.
620. Elegiac feelings American. New York: New Directions, 1970.

COSTANZO, Gerald
621. Badlands: first poems. Denver: Copper Canyon, 1973.

622. South moccasin. Orangeburg, SC: Peaceweed, 1973.

COTT, Jonathan
   623. Elective affinities. New York: Angel Hair, 1970.

COULETTE, Henri
   624. The attic. Ann Arbor, MI: University Microfilms, 1959.
   625. The war of the secret agents, and other poems. New York: Scribner, 1966.
   626. The family Goldschmitt. New York: Scribner, 1971.

COXE, Louis
   627. The sea faring. New York: Holt, 1947.
   628. The second man, and other poems. Minneapolis: University of Minnesota Press, 1955.
   629. The wilderness, and other poems. Minneapolis: University of Minnesota Press, 1958.
   630. The middle passage. Chicago: University of Chicago Press, 1960.
   631. The last hero, and other poems. Nashville: Vanderbilt University Press, 1965.
   632. Nikal seyn and decoration day. Nashville: Vanderbilt University Press, 1966.

CREELEY, Robert
   633. Le fou. Columbus, Ohio: Golden Goose, 1952.
   634. The kind of act of. Majorca: Divers, 1953.
   635. All that is lovely in men. Highlands, NC: Jargon, 1955.
   636. If you. San Francisco: Porpoise, 1956.
   637. The immoral proposition. Highlands, NC: J. Williams, 1957.
   638. The whip. Highlands, NC: Jargon, 1957.
   639. A form of women. New York: Jargon, 1959.
   640. For love; poems, 1950-1960. New York: Scribner, 1962.
   641. Poems, 1950-1965. London: Calder and Boyars, 1966.
   642. The charm: early and uncollected poems. Madison, WI: Perishable Press, 1967.
   643. Words. New York: Scribner, 1967.
   644. Divisions & other early poems. Madison, WI: Perishable Press, 1968.
   645. The finger. Los Angeles: Black Sparrow, 1968.
   646. Pieces. Los Angeles: Black Sparrow, 1968.
   647. 5 numbers. New York: Poets Press, 1969.
   648. As now it would be snow. 1970.
   649. In London. New York: Angel Hair, 1970.
   650. St. Martin's. Los Angeles: Black Sparrow, 1971.
   651. A day book. New York: Scribner, 1972.
   652. Gold diggers. New York: Scribner, 1972.
   653. Listen. Los Angeles: Black Sparrow, 1972.

CREWS, Judson
  654. Psalms for a late season. New Orleans: Iconograph,
     1942.
  655. No is the night. Taos, NM: privately printed, 1949.
  656. The anatomy of Proserpine. Ranches of Taos, NM,
     1955.
  657. The wrath wrenched splendor of love. Ranches of Taos,
     NM, 1956.
  658. The heart in naked hunger. Ranches of Taos, NM, 1958.
  659. The ogres who were his henchmen. Eureka, CA:
     Hearse, 1958.
  660. Inwade to Briney Garth. Taos, NM: Este Es, 1960.
  661. The feel of sun and air upon her body. Eureka, CA:
     Hearse, 1960.
  662. Hermes past the hour. Taos, NM: Este Es, 1963.
  663. A unicorn when needs be. Taos, NM: Este Es, 1963.
  664. Selected poems. Cleveland: Renegade, 1964.
  665. You, Mark Anthony. Taos, NM: Este Es, 1964.
  666. Angels fall they are towers. Taos, NM: Este Es, 1965.
  667. The stones of Kanorak. Santa Fe, NM: American
     Poets, 1966.

CROUCH, Stanley
  668. Ain't no ambulances for no nigguhs tonight. New York:
     R. W. Baron, 1972.

CRUZ, Victor
  669. Papo got his gun. New York: Calle Once, 1966.
  670. Snaps. New York: Random House, 1969.
  671. Mainland. New York: Random House, 1973.

CUNNINGHAM, J. V.
  672. The helmsman. San Francisco: Colt, 1942.
  673. The judge is fury. New York: Morrow, 1947.
  674. Doctor Drink. Cummington, MA: Cummington, 1950.
  675. The exclusions of a rhyme: poems and epigrams.
     Denver: Swallow, 1960.
  676. To what strangers, what welcome. Denver: Swallow,
     1964.
  677. Some salt. Madison, WI: Perishable Press, 1967.
  678. The collected poems and epigrams of J. V. Cunningham.
     Chicago: Swallow; London: Faber, 1971.

CURRY, Andrew
  679. 17th tractatus on words: selected poems. Paradise,
     CA: Dustbooks, 1969.

CURRY, David
  680. Here; poems, 1965-1969. New York: New Rivers, 1970.
  681. Theatre. Crete, NE: Best Cellar, 1973.

CUTLER, Bruce
  682. The year of the green waye. Lincoln: University of

Nebraska Press, 1960.
683. A west wind rises. Lincoln: University of Nebraska
      Press, 1962.
684. Sun City; sixteen poems and a translation. Lincoln:
      University of Nebraska Press, 1964.
685. A voyage to America, and other poems. Lincoln: Uni-
      versity of Nebraska Press, 1967.

D'ABATE, Richard
686. To keep the house from falling in. Ithaca, NY: Ithaca
      House, 1973.

DACEY, Philip
687. Fish, sweet giraffe, the lion, snake & owl. Poquoson,
      VA: Back Door, 1970.

DAHLBERG, Edward
688. Cipango's hinder door. Austin: University of Texas
      Press, 1965.
689. The sorrows of Priapus; consisting of The sorrows of
      Priapus and The carnal myth. New York: Harcourt,
      Brace, 1972.

D'AMBROSIO, Vinnie-Marie
690. Life of touching mouths. New York: New York Univer-
      sity Press, 1971.

DANA, Robert
691. My glass brother. Iowa City: Stone Wall, 1957.
692. The dark flags of waking. Iowa City: Quara, 1964.
693. Journeys from the skin. Iowa City: Hundred Pound
      Press, 1966.
694. Some versions of silence. New York: Norton, 1967.
695. The power of the visible. Chicago: Swallow, 1971.

DANN, Jack
696. Christs and other poems. Binghamton, NY: Bellevue
      Press, 1972.

DANNER, Margaret
697. To flower. Nashville: Counterpoise Series, 1963.
698. Iron lace. New York: Poets Press, 1968.

DARR, Ann
699. St. Ann's gut. New York: Morrow, 1971.
700. The myth of a woman's fist. New York: Morrow, 1973.

DAVIS, Glover
701. Bandaging bread. Iowa City: Cummington, 1971.

DAVISON, Peter
   702. The breaking of the day, and other poems.   New Haven:
           Yale University Press, 1964.
   703. The city and the island. New York: Atheneum, 1966.
   704. Pretending to be asleep. New York: Atheneum, 1970.
   705. Dark houses. Cambridge, MA: H. Ferguson, 1971.

DAWSON, Robert
   706. Six mile corner. Boston: Houghton Mifflin, 1966.

DEAN, Abner
   707. Wake me when it's over. New York: Simon and
           Schuster, 1955.
   708. Not far from the jungle. Cleveland: World, 1956.

DEEMER, Bill
   709. Poems. San Francisco: Auerhahn, 1964.
   710. Diana. San Francisco: Coyote Books, 1966.
   711. The king's bounty. Eugene, OR: privately printed,
           1968.
   712. A few for Lew. San Francisco: Tenth Muse, 1972.

DeFAZIO, Marjorie
   713. A quiet noise. New York: The Poets Press, 1972.

DEFFRY, Frank
   714. As near as i can tell. Chicago: Fenian Head Center,
           1969.
   715. Two states of mine (Texas and Louisiana). Sacramento:
           Hiatt, 1969.

DeFREES, Mary Madeline (Sister Mary Gilbert)
   716. From the darkroom. Indianapolis: Bobbs-Merrill, 1964.

DELL, William
   717. A benediction and other poems. Torrance, CA: Hors
           Commerce, 1967.
   718. Totem. Sacramento: Runcible Spoon, 1969.
   719. Cheeks. Sacramento: Runcible Spoon, 1969.

DeLONGCHAMPS, Joanne
   720. Eden under glass. Francestown, NH: Golden Quill,
           1957.
   721. The hungry lions. Bloomington: Indiana University
           Press, 1963.
   722. The wishing animal. Nashville: Vanderbilt University
           Press, 1970.

Den BOER, James
   723. Learning the way. Pittsburgh: University of Pittsburgh
           Press, 1968.
   724. Trying to come apart. Pittsburgh: University of Pitts-
           burgh Press, 1971.

725. Nine poems. Santa Barbara: Christopher's Press, 1972.

DENNEY, Reuel
726. The Connecticut River. New Haven: Yale University Press, 1939.
727. In praise of Adam. Chicago: University of Chicago Press, 1961.

DEPEW, Wally
728. Scream poem. Sacramento: Runcible Spoon, 1970.
729. Once. Paradise, CA: Dustbooks, 1971.

DeROCHE, Joseph
730. The inhabited scroll. Boston: Northeastern University Press, 1968.

DEUTCH, Richard
731. The dime. New York: New Rivers, 1970.

DICKEY, James
732. Into the stone. New York: Scribner, 1960.
733. Drowning with others. Middletown, CT: Wesleyan University Press, 1962.
734. Helmets. Middletown, CT: Wesleyan University Press, 1964.
735. Two poems of the air. Portland, OR: Centicore, 1964.
736. Buckdancer's choice. Middletown, CT: Wesleyan University Press, 1965.
737. Poems, 1957-1967. Middletown, CT: Wesleyan University Press, and London: Rapp & Carroll, 1967.
738. The eye-beaters, blood, victory, madness, Buckhead, and mercy. Garden City, NY: Doubleday, 1970.

DICKEY, R. P.
739. Running lucky. Chicago: Swallow, 1969.
740. Acting immortal. Columbia: University of Missouri Press, 1970.
741. Concise dictionary of Lead River, MO. Taos, NM: Black Bear, 1973.

DICKEY, William
742. Of the festivity. New Haven: Yale University Press, 1959.
743. Interpreter's house. Columbus: Ohio State University Press, 1963.
744. Rivers of the Pacific Northwest. San Francisco: Two-windows, 1969.
745. More under Saturn. Middletown, CT: Wesleyan University Press, 1971.

DILLARD, R. H. W.
746. The day I stopped dreaming about Barbara Steele, and

other poems.   Chapel Hill: University of North
Carolina Press, 1966.
747.   News of the Nile.   Chapel Hill: University of North
Carolina Press, 1971.
748.   After Borges.   Baton Rouge: Louisiana State University
Press, 1972.

DiPALMA, Ray
749.   Between the shapes.   East Lansing, MI: Zeitgeist, 1970.
750.   Clinches.   Madison, WI: Abraxas, 1970.
751.   The gallery goers.   Ithaca, NY: Ithaca House, 1971.
752.   All bowed down.   Providence, RI: Burning Deck, 1972.

DiPRIMA, Diane
753.   This kind of bird flies backward.   New York: Totem,
1958.
754.   The new handbook of heaven.   San Francisco: Auerhahn,
1963.
755.   Poems for Freddie.   New York: Poets Press, 1966.
756.   Haiku.   Topanga, CA: Love Press, 1967.
757.   Earthsong; poems, 1957-1959.   New York: Poets Press,
1968.
758.   Kerhonkson Journal.   Berkeley: Oyez, 1971.
759.   Revolutionary letters, etc.   San Francisco: City Lights,
1971.

DOBYNS, Stephen
760.   Concurring beasts.   New York: Atheneum, 1971.

DODSON, Owen
761.   Powerful long ladder.   New York: Farrar, Straus, 1946.
762.   The confession stone.   Detroit: Broadside, 1970.

DORBIN, Sanford M.
763.   Family life, and others.   Santa Barbara: Unicorn, 1968.
764.   The ruby woods.   Santa Barbara: White Rabbit/Open
Space, 1971.

DORESKI, William
765.   To face the sea.   Peterborough, NH: Windy Row Press,
1969.
766.   Running the bitch down.   Boston: Barn Dream, 1970.

DORMAN, Sonya
767.   Poems.   Columbus: Ohio State University Press, 1970.

DORN, Edward
768.   The newly fallen.   New York: Totem, 1961.
769.   From Gloucester out.   1964.
770.   Hands up!   New York: Totem, 1964.
771.   Idaho out.   1965.
772.   Geography.   London: Fulcrum, 1967.
773.   The North Atlantic turbine.   London: Fulcrum, 1967.

774. Gunslinger. Los Angeles: Black Sparrow, 1968.
775. Gunslinger, book II. Los Angeles: Black Sparrow, 1969.
776. Twenty-four love songs. San Francisco: Frontier, 1969.
777. Gunslinger 1 & 2. London: Fulcrum, 1970.
778. Songs set two: a short count. San Francisco: Frontier, 1970.
779. By the sound. San Francisco: Frontier, 1971.
780. The cycle. San Francisco: Frontier, 1971.
781. Some business recently transacted in the white world. San Francisco: Frontier, 1971.
782. Gunslinger, book III. San Francisco: Frontier, 1972.

DRAKE, Albert Dee
783. Pomes. Okemos, MI: Stone, 1972.

DREWRY, Carleton
784. A time of turning. New York: Dutton, 1951.
785. The writhen wood. New York: Dutton, 1953.
786. Cloud above clocktime. New York: Dutton, 1957.

DRUMMOND, Donald F.
787. No moat, no castle. Denver: Swallow, 1949.
788. The battlement. Denver: Swallow, 1956.
789. The drawbridge. Denver: Swallow, 1962.
790. The grey tower. Denver: Swallow, 1966.
791. The mountain. Chicago: Swallow, 1971.

DUBIE, Norman
792. Alehouse sonnets. Pittsburgh: University of Pittsburgh Press, 1971.

DUFAULT, Peter Kane
793. Angel of accidence. New York: Macmillan, 1954.
794. For some stringed instrument. New York: Macmillan, 1957.

DUGAN, Alan
795. Poems. New Haven: Yale University Press, 1961.
796. Poems 2. New Haven: Yale University Press, 1963.
797. Poems 3. New Haven: Yale University Press, 1967.
798. Collected poems. New Haven: Yale University Press, 1969; London: Faber, 1970.

DULL, Harold
799. The star year. Santa Barbara: White Rabbit/Open Space, 1967.

DUMAS, Gerald
800. An afternoon in Waterloo Park; a narrative poem. Boston: Houghton Mifflin, 1972.

DUMAS, Henry see CHATFIELD, Hale

DUNCAN, Robert
- 801. Heavenly city, earthly city. Berkeley: Bern Porter, 1947.
- 802. Poems: 1948-1949. Berkeley: Berkeley Miscellany, 1949.
- 803. Medieval scenes. San Francisco: Centaur, 1950.
- 804. Song of the Borderguard. Black Mountain, NC: Black Mountain College, 1952.
- 805. Caesar's gate. Majorca: Divers, 1955.
- 806. Letters: Poems 1953-1956. Highlands, NC: Jargon, 1958.
- 807. Selected poems. San Francisco: City Lights, 1959.
- 808. The opening of the field. New York: Grove, 1960; London: Cape, 1969.
- 809. Roots and branches. New York: Scribner, 1964; London: Cape, 1970.
- 810. Wine. Berkeley: Oyez, 1964.
- 811. A book of resemblances, 1950-1953. New Haven: H. Wenning, 1966.
- 812. Fragments of a disordered devotion. San Francisco: Gnomen, 1966.
- 813. Passages, 22-27. Berkeley: Oyez, 1966.
- 814. The years as catches; first poems, 1939-1946. Berkeley: Oyez, 1966.
- 815. Bending the bow. New York: New Directions, 1968.
- 816. Derivations: selected poems, vol. 2. London: Fulcrum, 1968.
- 817. The first decade: selected poems, vol. 1. London: Fulcrum, 1968.
- 818. Names of people. Los Angeles: Black Sparrow, 1968.
- 819. Achilles' song. New York: Phoenix Book Shop, 1969.
- 820. Tribunals: passages 31-35. Los Angeles: Black Sparrow, 1970.
- 821. The truth and life of myth. Fremont, MI: Sumac, 1972.
- 822. Opening of the field. Rev. ed., New York: New Directions, 1973.

DUNN, Joe
- 823. The better dream house. Santa Barbara: White Rabbit/ Open Space, 1968.

DUREM, Ray
- 824. Take no prisoners. Detroit: Broadside, 1971.

DUSENBERY, Gail
- 825. The mark. Berkeley: Oyez, 1967.
- 826. The sea-gull. Berkeley: Oyez, 1968.
- 827. The Bhengra dance. Berkeley: Oyez, 1970.

DUSENBERY, Walter
- 828. The story of the bed. Santa Barbara: White Rabbit/ Open Space, 1970.

EASTLAKE, William
829. A child's garden of verses for the revolution. New
       York: Grove, 1970.

EATON, Charles Edward
830. The bright plain. Chapel Hill: University of North
       Carolina Press, 1942.
831. The shadow of the swimmer. New York: Fine Editions,
       1951.
832. The greenhouse in the garden. New York: Twayne,
       1955.
833. Countermoves. New York: Abelard-Schuman, 1962;
       London: Abelard-Schuman, 1963.
834. On the edge of the knife. New York and London:
       Abelard-Schuman, 1970.

EBERHART, Richard
835. A bravery of earth. London: Cape, 1930; New York:
       Cape-Smith, 1931.
836. Reading the spirit. London: Chatto and Windus, 1936;
       New York: Oxford University Press, 1937.
837. A world-view. Medford, MA: Tufts College Press,
       1941.
838. Song and idea. London: Chatto and Windus, 1940; New
       York: Oxford University Press, 1942.
839. Poems, new and selected. New York: New Directions,
       1944.
840. Burr oaks. New York: Oxford University Press and
       London: Chatto and Windus, 1947.
841. Brotherhood of men. Pawlet, VT: Banyan, 1949.
842. An herb basket. Cummington, MA: Cummington, 1950.
843. Selected poems. New York: Oxford University Press,
       and London: Chatto and Windus, 1951.
844. Undercliff; poems, 1946-1953. New York: Oxford Uni-
       versity Press, and London: Chatto and Windus, 1953.
845. Great praises. New York: Oxford University Press,
       and London: Chatto and Windus, 1957.
846. The oak. Hanover, NH: Pine Tree Press, 1957.
847. Collected poems, 1930-1960. New York: Oxford Uni-
       versity Press, and London: Chatto and Windus, 1960.
848. The quarry. New York: Oxford University Press, and
       London: Chatto and Windus, 1964.
849. Selected poems, 1930-1965. New York: New Directions,
       1965.
850. Thirty one sonnets. New York: Eakins, 1967.
851. Shifts of being. New York: Oxford University Press,
       and London: Chatto and Windus, 1968.
852. Three poems. Cambridge, MA: Pym-Randall, 1968.
853. Fields of grace. New York: Oxford University Press,
       1972.

EBON (Ebon Dooley)
854. Revolution. Chicago: Third World, 1968.

ECKELS, Jon
855. Black right on. San Francisco: J. Richardson, 1969.
856. Home is where the soul is. Detroit: Broadside, 1969.
857. Our business in the streets; Black poetry. Detroit: Broadside, 1971.

ECKMAN, Frederick
858. Sandusky & black: new and selected poems. New Rochelle, NY: Elizabeth, 1970.

ECONOMOU, George
859. The georgics. Los Angeles: Black Sparrow, 1968.
860. Landed natures. Los Angeles: Black Sparrow, 1969.
861. Poems for self therapy. Madison, WI: Perishable Press, 1972.

EDELMAN, Richard Wayne
862. The wedding feast. Berkeley: Oyez, 1970.

EDSON, Russell
863. What a man can see. New York: Jargon, 1969.
864. The childhood of an equestrian. New York: Harper & Row, 1972.
865. The clam theater. Middletown, CT: Wesleyan University Press, 1973.

EIGNER, Larry
866. From the sustaining air. Majorca: Divers, 1953.
867. Look at the park. Lynn, MA: privately printed, 1959.
868. On my eyes. Highlands, NC: J. Williams, 1960.
869. The music, the rooms. Santa Fe, NM: Desert Review Press, 1966.
870. Another time in fragments. London: Fulcrum, 1967.
871. The--/Towards Autumn. Los Angeles: Black Sparrow, 1967.
872. Six poems. Portland, OR: Wine Press, 1967.
873. Air; the trees. Los Angeles: Black Sparrow, 1968.
874. The breath of once live things; in the field with Poe. Los Angeles: Black Sparrow, 1968.
875. A line that may be cut. London: Circle, 1968.
876. Valleys/branches. London: Big Venus, 1969.
877. Selected poems. Berkeley: Oyez, 1972.
878. Words touching ground under. Belmont, MA: Hellric, 1973.

ELLIOTT, George P.
879. Fever and chills. Iowa City: Stone Wall, 1961.
880. From the Berkeley hills. New York: Harper & Row, 1969.

ELLIOTT, Harley
881. Dark country. Trumansburg, NY: Crossing Press, 1971.

ELMSLIE, Kenward
  882. Pavilions. New York: Tibor de Nagy, 1961.
  883. Power plant poems. New York: "C" Press, 1967.
  884. The champ. Los Angeles: Black Sparrow, 1968.
  885. Album. New York: Kulchur, 1969.
  886. Circus nerves. Los Angeles: Black Sparrow, 1971.
  887. Girl machine. New York: Angel Hair, 1971.
  888. Motor disturbance. New York: Columbia University
      Press, 1971.

EL MUHAJIR see X, Marvin and Jackmon, Marvin

EMANUEL, James A.
  889. The treehouse, and other poems. Detroit: Broadside,
      1968.
  890. Panther man. Detroit: Broadside, 1970.

ENGELS, John
  891. The Homer Mitchell place. Pittsburgh: University of
      Pittsburgh Press, 1968.

ENGLE, Paul
  892. Worn earth. New Haven: Yale University Press, 1932.
  893. American song. Garden City, NY: Doubleday, 1934.
  894. Break the heart's anger. Garden City, NY: Doubleday,
      1936.
  895. Corn. Garden City, NY: Doubleday, 1939.
  896. West of midnight. New York: Random House, 1941.
  897. American child. New York: Random House, 1945.
  898. The word of love. New York: Random House, 1951.
  899. American child; sonnets for my daughters, with thirty-
      six new poems. New York: Dial, 1956.
  900. For the Iowa dead. Iowa City: State University of
      Iowa Press, 1956.
  901. Poems in praise. New York: Random House, 1959.
  902. An old-fashioned Christmas. New York: Longmans
      Green, 1962.
  903. A prairie Christmas. New York: Longmans Green,
      1962.
  904. A woman unashamed. New York: Random House, 1965.
  905. Embrace; selected love poems. New York: Random
      House, 1969.

ENGLISH, Maurice
  906. Midnight in the century. Denver: Swallow, 1964.

ENSLIN, Theodore
  907. The work proposed. Kyoto: Origin, 1958.
  908. New Sharon's prospect. Kyoto: Origin, 1962.
  909. The place where I am standing. New Rochelle, NY:
      Elizabeth, 1964.
  910. New Sharon's prospect and journals. San Francisco:
      Coyote's Journal, 1966.

911. This do & the talents. Mexico City: El Corno Em-
      plumado, 1966.
912. To come to have become. New Rochelle, NY: Eliza-
      beth, 1966.
913. Characters in certain places. Portland, OR: Prensa
      de Lagar, 1967.
914. The diabelli variations. Annandale-on-Hudson, NY:
      Matter Books, 1967.
915. Agreement and back. New Rochelle, NY: Elizabeth,
      1968.
916. 2/30-6/31. Cabot, VT: Vermont Stoveside, 1968.
917. Forms, part I: the first dimensions. New Rochelle,
      NY: Elizabeth, 1970.
918. The poems. New Rochelle, NY: Elizabeth, 1970.
919. The country of our consciousness. Berkeley: Sand
      Dollar, 1971.
920. Etudes. New Rochelle, NY: Elizabeth, 1972.
921. Forms, part II: the Tessaract. New Rochelle, NY:
      Elizabeth, 1971.
922. Forms, part III: the experiences. New Rochelle, NY:
      Elizabeth, 1972.
923. Forms, part IV: the fusion. New Rochelle, NY:
      Elizabeth, 1972.
924. Views. New Rochelle, NY: Elizabeth, 1973.
925. With light reflected. Fremont, MI: Sumac, 1973.

EPSTEIN, Daniel Mark
926. No vacancies in hell. New York: Liveright, 1973.

ESHLEMAN, Clayton
927. Mexico and north. Tokyo: privately printed, 1961.
928. The chavin illumination. Lima, Peru: La Rama Florida,
      1965.
929. Lachrymae mateo. New York: Caterpillar, 1967.
930. Walks. New York: Caterpillar, 1967
931. Brother stones. New York: Caterpillar, 1968.
932. Cantaloups & splendor. Los Angeles: Black Sparrow,
      1968.
933. The house of Okumura. Toronto: Weed/Flower, 1968.
934. Indiana. Los Angeles: Black Sparrow, 1969.
935. The house of Ibuki: a poem. New York City, 14 March-
      30 Sept. 1967. La Grosse, WI: Sumac, 1969.
936. A pitchblende. San Francisco: Mayo Quarto, 1969.
937. Yellow River record. London: Big Venus, 1969.
938. Altars. Los Angeles: Black Sparrow, 1971.
939. Bearings. Santa Barbara: Capricorn, 1971.
940. Coils. Los Angeles: Black Sparrow, 1973.

ESLER, Richard
941. Exits and entrances. Pittsburgh: University of Pitts-
      burgh Press, 1961.

ETTER, Dave
  942. Go read the river. Lincoln: University of Nebraska
      Press, 1966.
  943. The last train to Prophetstown. Lincoln: University of
      Nebraska Press, 1968.
  944. Voyages to the inland sea. Madison, WI: University of
      Wisconsin Press, 1971.

EVANS, Abbie Huston
  945. The bright north. New York: Macmillan, 1938.
  946. Fact of crystal. New York: Harcourt, Brace, 1961.
  947. The collected poems. Pittsburgh: University of Pitts-
      burgh Press, 1970.

EVANS, Mari
  948. Where is all the music? London: Breman, 1968.
  949. I am a Black woman. New York: Morrow, 1970.
  950. JD. New York: Doubleday, 1973.

EVERSON, William O. see ANTONINUS, Brother

EVERWINE, Peter
  951. Collecting the animals. New York: Atheneum, 1973.

FABILLI, Mary
  952. The old ones. Berkeley: Oyez, 1966.
  953. Aurora Bligh & early poems. Berkeley: Oyez, 1968.

FAGIN, Larry
  954. Parade of the caterpillars. New York: Angel Hair,
      1968.
  955. 12 poems. New York: Angel Hair, 1972.

FARLEY, Jean
  956. Figure and field. Chapel Hill: University of North
      Carolina Press, 1970.

FEARING, Kenneth
  957. Angel arms. New York: Coward McCann, 1929.
  958. Poems. New York: Dynamo, 1935.
  959. Dead reckoning. New York: Random House, 1938.
  960. Collected poems. New York: Random House, 1940.
  961. Afternoon of a pawnbroker. New York: Harcourt,
      Brace, 1943.
  962. Stranger at Coney Island. New York: Harcourt, Brace,
      1948.
  963. New and selected poems. Bloomington: Indiana Univer-
      sity Press, 1956.

FEINBERG, Harvey
  964. Cock of the morning. Trumansburg, NY: Crossing
      Press, 1971.

FELD, Ross
965. Plum poems. New York: Jargon, 1972.

FELDMAN, Irving
966. Works and days. Boston: Little, Brown, and London: Deutsch, 1961.
967. The pripet marshes. New York: Viking, 1965.
968. Cosmos. New York: Harper & Row, 1970.
969. Magic papers. New York: Harper & Row, 1970.
970. Lost originals. Holt, Rinehart, and Winston, 1972.

FERLINGHETTI, Lawrence
971. Pictures of the gone world. San Francisco: City Lights, 1955.
972. A Coney Island of the mind. New York: New Directions, 1958.
973. Tentative description of a dinner given to promote the impeachment of President Eisenhower. San Francisco: Golden Mountain, 1958.
974. Berlin. San Francisco: Golden Mountain, 1961.
975. One thousand fearful words for Fidel Castro. San Francisco: City Lights, 1961.
976. Starting from San Francisco. Norfolk, CT: New Directions, 1961.
977. Where is Vietnam? San Francisco: City Lights, 1965.
978. An eye on the world. London: MacGibbon and Kee, 1967.
979. After the cries of the birds. San Francisco: D. Haselwood Books, 1967.
980. Moscow in the wilderness, Segovia in the snow. San Francisco: Beach Books, 1967.
981. Starting from San Francisco. Enl. ed. New York: New Directions, 1967.
982. The secret meaning of things. New York: New Directions, 1969.
983. Tyrannus Nix. New York: New Directions, 1969.
984. Back roads to far places. New York: New Directions, 1971.
985. Open eye, open heart. New York: New Directions, 1973.

FERRY, David
986. On the way to the island. Middletown, CT: Wesleyan University Press, 1960.

FIELD, Edward
987. Stand up, friend, with me. New York: Grove, 1963.
988. Variety photoplays. New York: Grove, 1967.

FIELDS, Julia
989. Poems. Millbrook, NY: Kriya, 1968.

FIELDS, Kenneth
    990. Sunbelly. Boston: Godine, 1973.

FIGUEROA, Jose-Angel
    991. East 110th Street. Detroit: Broadside, 1972.

FINKEL, Donald
    992. The clothing's new emperor. New York: Scribner,
          1959.
    993. Simeon. New York: Atheneum, 1964.
    994. A joyful noise. New York: Atheneum, 1966.
    995. Answer back. New York: Atheneum, 1968.
    996. The garbage wars. New York: Atheneum, 1970.
    997. Adequate earth. New York: Atheneum, 1972.

FINSTEIN, Max
    998. Savonarola's tune. New York: Totem, 1959.
    999. The disappearance of mountains; poems, 1960-63. San
          Francisco: Wild Dog, 1966.
   1000. There's always a moon in America. San Francisco:
          Cranium, 1968.

FITZELL, Lincoln
   1001. Selected poems. Denver: Swallow, 1955.

FITZGERALD, Robert
   1002. Poems. New York: Arrow Editions, 1935.
   1003. A wreath for the sea. New York: Arrow Editions and
          New Directions, 1943.
   1004. In the rose of time; poems, 1931-1956. New York:
          New Directions, 1956.
   1005. Spring shade; poems, 1931-1970. New York: New
          Directions, 1971.

FITZSIMMONS, Thomas
   1006. Meditation seeds. Ithaca, NY: Stone Marrow, 1971.
   1007. Playseeds. Grand Rapids, MI: Pilot, 1973.

FIXEL, Lawrence
   1008. The scale of silence. Santa Cruz, CA: Kayak, 1969.

FLAHERTY, Douglas
   1009. The elderly battlefield nurse. Albuquerque: Road
          Runner, 1968.
   1010. Weaving a slow dream of hands. Dublin: Seafront,
          1972.

FLANAGAN, Robert
   1011. Not for Dietrich Bonhoeffer. Trumansburg, NY: New/
          Books, 1969.
   1012. Body. Toronto: House of Anansi, 1970.

FORD, Charles Henri
  1013. The garden of disorder. Norfolk, CT: New Directions,
         1938.
  1014. ABC's. Prairie City, IL: Decker, 1940.
  1015. Overturned lake. Cincinnati: Little Man, 1941.
  1016. Sleep in a nest of flames. Norfolk, CT: New Direc-
         tions, 1949.
  1017. Spare parts. New York: New View Books, 1966.
  1018. Flag of ecstasy. Los Angeles: Black Sparrow, 1972.

FORD, Gena
  1019. Tall tales from far corners. New Rochelle, NY:
         Elizabeth, 1962.
  1020. A planting of chives. New Rochelle, NY: Elizabeth,
         1964.
  1021. This time, that space. New Rochelle, NY: Elizabeth,
         1968.
  1022. Homesickness for big men. New Rochelle, NY: Eliza-
         beth, 1972.

FORREST, Bernard A.
  1023. Titled and untitled. Torrance, CA: Hors Commerce,
         1965.
  1024. There are birds in the computer. Torrance, CA:
         Hors Commerce, 1967.
  1025. Not all I see is there. Los Angeles: Black Sparrow,
         1970.

FOSTER, Charles
  1026. Victoria Mundi. New York: The Smith, 1973.

FOWLER, Gene
  1027. Field studies. El Cerrito, CA: Dustbooks, 1965.
  1028. Quarter tones. Grande Ronde, OR: G.R.R., 1966.
  1029. Shaman songs. El Cerrito, CA: Dustbooks, 1967.
  1030. Fires. New York: Grove, 1969.
  1031. Her Majesty's ship. Sacramento, CA: G.R.R., 1969.

FOWLER, Hilary
  1032. Mind dances. Paradise, CA: Dustbooks, 1966.
  1033. Colors; street poems. Sacramento: Runcible Spoon,
         1968.

FOX, Hugh
  1034. Eye into now; a series of poem scripts. Los Angeles:
         Ediciones de la Frontera, 1967.
  1035. Soul-catcher songs. Los Angeles: Ediciones de la
         Frontera, 1967.
  1036. Apotheosis of Olde Towne. San Bruno, CA: Fat Frog,
         1968.

FOX, Siv Cedering
  1037. Cup of cold water. New York: New Rivers, 1973.

1038.   Letters from the island.   Fredericton, NB, Canada:
        Fiddlehead, 1973.

FRANCIS, Robert
1039.   Stand with me here.   New York: Macmillan, 1936.
1040.   Valhalla and other poems.   New York: Macmillan,
        1938.
1041.   The sound I listened for.   New York: Macmillan, 1944.
1042.   The face against the glass.   Amherst, MA: privately
        printed, 1950.
1043.   The orb weaver.   Middletown, CT: Wesleyan Univer-
        sity Press, 1960.
1044.   Come out into the sun.   Amherst: University of Massa-
        chusetts Press, 1965.

FRASER, Kathleen
1045.   Change of address.   San Francisco: Kayak, 1966.
1046.   In defiance of the rain.   Santa Cruz, CA: Kayak, 1969.
1047.   Trying to live on Liberty Street.   New York: Harper
        & Row, 1973.
1048.   What I want.   New York: Harper & Row, 1973.

FREEMAN, Arthur
1049.   Apollonian poems.   New York: Atheneum, 1961.
1050.   Estrangements.   New York: Harcourt, Brace, 1966.
1051.   Assays of bias.   Boston: Godine, 1970.

FRIEBERT, Stuart
1052.   Dreaming of floods.   Nashville: Vanderbilt University
        Press, 1969.

FROST, Richard
1053.   The circus villains.   Athens: Ohio University Press,
        1965.
1054.   Getting drunk with the birds.   Athens: Ohio University
        Press, 1971.

FRUMKIN, Gene
1055.   The hawk and the lizard.   Denver: Swallow, 1963.
1056.   Dostoyevsky & other nature poems.   San Luis Obispo,
        CA: Solo, 1972.
1057.   Locust cry/poems: 1958-1965.   Los Cerrillos, NM:
        San Marcos, 1973.

FULLER, Stephany
1058.   Moving deep.   Detroit: Broadside, 1970.

FULLER, Winston
1059.   Twelve poems.   Pittsburgh: Hoechstetter, 1972.

FULTON, Robin
1060.   Blok's twelve.   Preston, Lancs.: Akros Publications,
        1968.

1061.   The spaces between the stones is where the survivors
        live. New York: New Rivers, 1971.

GALE, Vi
    1062.   Several houses. Denver: Swallow, 1959.
    1063.   Love always. Denver: Swallow, 1965.
    1064.   Clouded sea. Portland, OR: Press 22, 1971.

GALL, Gretchen
    1065.   Touch earth. Vermillion: University of South Dakota
            Press, 1973.

GALLER, David
    1066.   Walls and distances. New York: Macmillan, 1959.
    1067.   Leopards in the temple. New York: Macmillan, 1968.

GALLUP, Dick
    1068.   Hinges. New York: "C" Press, 1965.
    1069.   Where I hang my hat. New York: Harper & Row,
            1970.

GALT, John
    1070.   The common ground. Denver: Verb, 1964.

GALT, Lisa
    1071.   Radar. Sacramento: Runcible Spoon, 1966.

GANGEMI, Kenneth.
    1072.   Lydia. Los Angeles: Black Sparrow, 1970.

GARCIA, Luis
    1073.   Mister menu. Santa Cruz, CA: Kayak, 1967.

GARDNER, Isabella
    1074.   Birthdays from the ocean. Boston: Houghton Mifflin,
            1955.
    1075.   The looking glass. Chicago: University of Chicago
            Press, 1961.
    1076.   West of childhood; poems, 1950-1965. Boston:
            Houghton Mifflin, 1965.

GARDONS, S. S. see SNODGRASS, W. D.

GARRETT, George
    1077.   The reverend ghost. New York: Scribner, 1957.
    1078.   The sleeping gypsy. Austin: University of Texas
            Press, 1958.
    1079.   Abraham's knife. Chapel Hill: University of North
            Carolina Press, 1961.
    1080.   For a bitter season; new and selected poems. Colum-
            bia: University of Missouri Press, 1967.

GARRIGUE, Jean
   1081. The ego and the centaur. New York: New Directions, 1947.
   1082. The monument rose. New York: Noonday, 1953.
   1083. A water walk by Villa d'Este. New York: St. Martin's, 1959.
   1084. Country without maps. New York: Macmillan, 1964.
   1085. New and selected poems. New York: Macmillan, 1967.
   1086. Chartres, & prose poems. New York: Eakins, 1971.
   1087. Studies for an actress. New York: Macmillan, 1973.

GAVRONSKY, Serge
   1088. Poems and texts. New York: October House, 1969.

GEOGAKAS, Dan
   1089. And all living things their children. San Lorenzo, CA: Shameless Hussy, 1972.

GERBER, Dan
   1090. The waiting. Philadelphia: Dorrance, 1966.
   1091. The revenant. Fremont, MI: Sumac, 1971.
   1092. Departure. Fremont, MI: Sumac, 1973.

GHISELIN, Brewster
   1093. Against the circle. New York: Dutton, 1946.
   1094. The nets. New York: Dutton, 1955.
   1095. Country of the Minotaur. Salt Lake City: University of Utah Press, 1970.

GIBBS, Barbara
   1096. The well. Denver: Swallow, 1941.
   1097. The green chapel. New York: Noonday, 1958.
   1098. Poems written in Berlin. Pawlet, VT: Claude Fredericks, 1959.
   1099. The meeting place of colors. West Branch, IA: Cummington, 1973.

GIBSON, Walker
   1100. The reckless spenders. Bloomington: Indiana University Press, 1954.
   1101. Come as you are. New York: Hastings House, 1958.

GILBERT, Jack
   1102. Views of jeopardy. New Haven: Yale University Press, 1962.
   1103. On my own hallelujahs. Chicago: Third World, 1971.

GILDNER, Gary
   1104. First practice. Pittsburgh: University of Pittsburgh Press, 1969.
   1105. Digging for Indians. Pittsburgh: University of Pittsburgh Press, 1971.

GILDZEN, Alex
    1106. Into the sea. Madison, WI: Abraxas, 1969.

GILFILLAN, Merrill
    1107. Truck. New York: Angel Hair, 1970.
    1108. Skyliner. Iowa City: Blue Wind, 1972.

GILL, John
    1109. Young man's letter. Trumansburg, NY: New/Books, 1967.
    1110. Gill's blues. Trumansburg, NY: Crossing Press, 1969.

GILLMAN, Richard
    1111. Too much alone. Denver: Swallow, 1965.

GILLON, Adam
    1112. Daily new and old; poems in the manner of haiku. New York: Astra Books, 1971.

GILMAN, Dugan
    1113. Upstate. Middletown, CT: Wesleyan University Press, 1971.

GINSBERG, Allen
    1114. Howl. San Francisco: City Lights, 1956.
    1115. Empty mirror. New York: Totem, 1961.
    1116. Kaddish, and other poems, 1958-1960. San Francisco: City Lights, 1961.
    1117. Reality sandwiches, 1953-60. San Francisco: City Lights, 1963.
    1118. Wichita vortex sutra. London: Housmans, 1966.
    1119. Ankor-Wat. London: Fulcrum, 1968.
    1120. Planet news, 1961-1967. San Francisco: City Lights, 1968.
    1121. T. V. baby poems. London: Cape Goliard, 1967; New York: Grossman, 1968.
    1122. Airplane dreams; compositions from journals. Toronto: Anansi, 1968; San Francisco: City Lights, 1969.
    1123. The fall of America: poems of these states, 1965-1971. San Francisco: City Lights, 1972.
    1124. The gates of wrath: rhymed poems, 1948-1952. Bolinas, CA: Grey Fox, 1972.

GIORNO, John
    1125. Poems. New York: Mother, 1967.
    1126. Balling Buddha. New York: Kulchur, 1970.
    1127. Birds. New York: Angel Hair, 1971.
    1128. Cancer in my left ball. Barton, VT: Something Else, 1973.

GIOVANNI, Nikki
    1129. Black judgment. Detroit: Broadside, 1968.
    1130. All I gotta do. Detroit: Broadside, 1970.
    1131. Black feeling, Black talk. Detroit: Broadside, 1970.

1132. Black feeling, Black talk, Black judgment. New York: Morrow, 1970.
1133. Re:creation. Detroit: Broadside, 1970.
1134. My house. New York: Morrow, 1972.

GLAZE, Andrew
1135. Damned ugly children. Los Angeles: Trident, 1966.

GLEASON, Madeline
1136. Poems 1944. San Francisco: Grabhorn, 1944.
1137. The metaphysical needle. San Francisco: Centaur, 1949.
1138. Concerto for bell and telephone. Santa Barbara: Unicorn, 1957.
1139. Selected poems. Georgetown, CA: Dragon's Teeth, 1972.

GLÜCK, Louise
1140. Firstborn. New York: World, 1968; London: Anvil Press, 1969.

GODSEY, Edwin
1141. Cabin fever. Chapel Hill: University of North Carolina Press, 1967.

GOEDICKE, Patricia
1142. Between oceans. New York: Harcourt, Brace, 1968.

GOLDBARTH, Albert
1143. Feces fruit. New York: New Rivers, 1973.
1144. Under cover. Crete, NE: Best Cellar, 1973.

GOLDENSOHN, Barry
1145. Saint Venus Eve. Iowa City: Cummington, 1973.

GOLDFARB, Sidney
1146. Speech, for instance. New York: Farrar, Straus, 1969.
1147. Messages. New York: Farrar, Straus, 1971.

GOLDMAN, Michael
1148. First poems. New York: Macmillan, 1965.
1149. At the edge. New York: Macmillan, 1969.

GOODMAN, Paul
1150. Stop-light. Harrington, NJ: 5x8 Press, 1942.
1151. The well of Bethlehem. New York: privately printed, n. d.
1152. Red Jacket. New York: privately printed, 1956.
1153. The lordly Hudson. New York: Macmillan, 1962.
1154. Day and other poems. New York: privately printed, 1965.
1155. Hawkweed. New York: Random House, 1967.

1156. North Percy. Los Angeles: Black Sparrow, 1968.
1157. Homespun of oatmeal gray. New York: Random House, 1970.
1158. Collected poems. New York: Random House, 1973.

GOODREAU, William
1159. The many islands. New York: Atheneum, 1961.
1160. In my Father's house. New York: Atheneum, 1964.

GOTTLIEB, Darcy
1161. No witness but ourselves. Columbia: University of Missouri Press, 1973.

GRAHAM, Le see ALHAMISI, Ahmed

GRAHAM, Robert
1162. The annals of Logan. New York: Holt, Rinehart and Winston, 1961.

GRAY, Darrell
1163. Excuses. Madison, WI: Abraxas, 1969.
1164. Space sonnets. Iowa City: Blue Wind, 1971.
1165. The beauties of travel. Bowling Green, OH: Doones, 1972.

GRAY, Don
1166. Little un's book. San Francisco: Twowindows, 1968.
1167. The outside silence of things. Folsom, CA: Grande Ronde, 1968.
1168. The five hours. San Francisco: Twowindows, 1969.
1169. Dark side of the moon. San Francisco: Twowindows, 1970.

GREBANIER, Bernard
1170. The other love, a triptych. New York: Bookman Associates, 1957.
1171. The angel in the rock. Georgetown, CA: Dragon's Teeth, 1971.

GREENBERG, Alvin
1172. The metaphysical giraffe. New York: New Rivers, 1968.
1173. The house of the would-be gardener. New York: New Rivers, 1972.
1174. Dark lands. Ithaca, NY: Ithaca House, 1973.

GREENE, Jonathan
1175. The reckoning. Annandale-on-Hudson, NY: Matter Books, 1966.
1176. Instance. Lexington, KY: Buttonwood, 1968.
1177. The lapidary. Los Angeles: Black Sparrow, 1969.
1178. A 17th century garner. Lexington, KY: Buttonwood, 1969.

GREENLEE, Sam
  1179. Blues for an African princess. Chicago: Third World,
        1971.

GREER, Scott A.
  1180. Via urbana. Denver: Swallow, 1963.

GREGOR, Arthur
  1181. Octavian shooting targets. New York: Dodd, Mead,
        1954.
  1182. 1, 2, 3, 4, 5. Philadelphia: Lippincott, 1956.
  1183. Declensions of a refrain. New York: Dodd, Mead,
        1957.
  1184. Basic movements. New York: Gure Press, 1966.
  1185. Figure in the door. Garden City, NY: Doubleday,
        1968.
  1186. A bed by the sea. Garden City, NY: Doubleday, 1970.
  1187. Selected poems. Garden City, NY: Doubleday, 1971.

GROLMES, Sam
  1188. After Oskosk. Sacramento: Runcible Spoon, 1969.
  1189. Moon poem. Sacramento: Runcible Spoon, 1969.

GROSS, Harvey
  1190. Plans for an orderly apocalypse. Ann Arbor: Univer-
        sity of Michigan Press, 1968.

GROSS, Ronald
  1191. Pop poems. New York: Simon and Schuster, 1967.

GROSVENOR, Kali
  1192. Poems by Kali. Garden City, NY: Doubleday, 1970.

GROSVENOR, Verta Mae
  1193. Thursdays and every other Sunday off. Garden City,
        NY: Doubleday, 1972.

GUEST, Barbara
  1194. Poems: The location of things, Archaics, The open
        skies. Garden City, NY: Doubleday, 1962.
  1195. The blue stairs. New York: Corinth, 1968.
  1196. Moscow mansions. New York: Viking, 1973.

GULLANS, Charles
  1197. Moral poems. Palo Alto, CA: John Hunter Thomas,
        1957.
  1198. Arrivals & departures. Minneapolis: University of
        Minnesota Press, 1962.

GUNDERSON, Keith
  1199. A continual interest in the sun and sea. London and
        New York: Abelard-Schuman, 1971.

HAAG, John
1200. The brine-breather. Santa Cruz, CA: Kayak, 1970.

HADLEY, Drummond
1201. The webbing. San Francisco: Four Seasons, 1967.
1202. The spirit by the deep well tank. Santa Fe, NM:
Goliard/Santa Fe, 1972.
1203. Strands of rawhide. Santa Fe, NM: Goliard/Santa Fe,
1972.

HAHN, Hannelore
1204. Taking a giant step. Boston: Little, Brown, 1960.

HAINES, John
1205. Winter news. Middletown, CT: Wesleyan University
Press, 1966.
1206. The mirror. Santa Barbara: Unicorn, 1971.
1207. The stone harp. Middletown, CT: Wesleyan Univer-
sity Press, 1971.
1208. Twenty poems. Santa Barbara: Unicorn, 1971.
1209. Leaves and ashes. Santa Cruz, CA: Kayak, 1973.

HAISLIP, John
1210. Not every year. Seattle: University of Washington
Press, 1971.

HALE, Janet Campbell
1211. Owl's song. Garden City, NY: Doubleday, 1973.

HALL, Carol
1212. Portrait of your niece. Minneapolis: University of
Minnesota Press, 1959.

HALL, D. J.
1213. Journey into morning. Middletown, CT: Wesleyan
University Press, 1973.

HALL, Donald
1214. Exiles and marriages. New York: Viking, 1955.
1215. To the loud wind. Cambridge: Harvard Advocate,
1955.
1216. The dark houses. New York: Viking, 1958.
1217. A roof of tiger lilies. New York: Viking, and London:
Deutsch, 1964.
1218. The alligator bride; poems new and selected. New
York: Harper & Row, 1969.
1219. The yellow room; love poems. New York: Harper &
Row, 1971.

HALL, J. C.
1220. A house of words. Middletown, CT: Wesleyan Uni-
versity Press, 1973.

HALL, James B.
1221. The hunt within. Baton Rouge: Louisiana State University Press, 1973.

HALL, Walter
1222. The music threat. Berkeley: Trask House, 1971.
1223. Blowing in the dark. Providence, RI: Burning Deck, 1973.

HALLEY, Anne
1224. Between wars. Amherst: University of Massachusetts Press, 1965.

HALPERN, Daniel
1225. Traveling on credit. New York: Viking, 1972.

HALPERN, Martin
1226. Two sides of an island. Chapel Hill: University of North Carolina Press, 1963.

HAMILTON, Alfred Starr
1227. Sphinx. Montclair, NJ: Kumquat, 1968.
1228. The selected poems of Alfred Starr Hamilton. Highlands, NC: Jargon, 1969.

HAMMER, Adam
1229. Magnito star mine. Boston: Barn Dream, 1973.

HAMMER, Louis
1230. Bone planet. San Francisco: Kayak, 1967.

HAMMOND, Mac
1231. The horse opera. Columbus: Ohio State University Press, 1966.
1232. Cold turkey. Chicago: Swallow, 1969.

HANNIGAN, Paul
1233. Holland and the Netherlands. Cambridge, MA: Pym-Randall, 1970.
1234. Laughing. Boston: Houghton Mifflin, 1970.
1235. The carnation. Boston: Barn Dream, 1972.

HANS, Marcie
1236. Serve me a slice of moon. New York: Harcourt, Brace, 1965.

HANSON, Karen
1237. Spine. Ithaca, NY: Ithaca House, 1971.

HANSON, Kenneth O.
1238. 8 poems /1958. Portland, OR: privately printed, 1958.
1239. The distance anywhere. Seattle: University of Washington Press, 1967.

1240. Saronikos and other poems. Portland, OR, 1972.
1241. The uncorrected world. Middletown, CT: Wesleyan University Press, 1973.

HANSON, Pauline
1242. The forever young. Denver: Swallow, 1948.
1243. The forever young and other poems. Denver: Swallow, 1957.
1244. Across countries of anywhere. New York: Knopf, 1971.

HARMON, William
1245. Treasury holiday; thirty-four fits for the opening of fiscal year 1968. Middletown, CT: Wesleyan University Press, 1970.
1246. Legion: civic courses. Middletown, CT: Wesleyan University Press, 1973.

HARNACK, Curtis
1247. We have all gone away. Garden City, NY: Doubleday, 1973.

HARPER, Michael S.
1248. Dear John, dear Coltrane. Pittsburgh: University of Pittsburgh Press, 1970.
1249. History is your own heartbeat. Urbana: University of Illinois Press, 1971.
1250. Song: I want a witness. Pittsburgh: University of Pittsburgh Press, 1972.
1251. Photographs: negatives: history as apple tree. San Francisco: Scarab, 1972.
1252. Debridement. Garden City, NY: Doubleday, 1973.

HARR, Barbara
1253. The mortgaged wife. Chicago: Swallow, 1970.

HARRISON, Jim
1254. Plain song. New York: Norton, 1965.
1255. Locations. New York: Norton, 1968.
1256. Outlyer and ghazals. New York: Simon and Schuster, 1971.
1257. Letters to Yesenin. Fremont, MI: Sumac, 1973.

HARROD, Elizabeth
1258. Seascape with snow. Denver: Swallow, 1960.

HARVEY, Mark
1259. A lady with a flute to be tuned. Ithaca, NY: Stone Marrow, 1971.

HARWOOD, Grace
1260. Half a loaf. San Francisco: Peace & Pieces, 1973.

HARWOOD, Lee
   1261. The man with blue eyes. New York: Angel Hair, 1966.

HASS, Robert
   1262. Field guide. New Haven: Yale University Press, 1973.
   1263. Liveoak. New Haven: Yale University Press, 1973.

HATHAWAY, William
   1264. True confessions & false romances. Ithaca, NY:
       Ithaca House, 1972.

HAY, Sara Henderson
   1265. The delicate balance. New York: Scribner, 1951.
   1266. A footing on this earth. Garden City, NY: Doubleday,
       1966.

HAYDEN, Robert
   1267. Heartshape in the dust. Detroit: Falcon, 1940.
   1268. The lion and the archer. Nashville: Counterpoise,
       1948.
   1269. Figure of time. Nashville: Hemphill, 1955.
   1270. A ballad of remembrance. London: Bremen, 1962.
   1271. Selected poems. New York: October House, 1966.
   1272. Words in the mourning time. New York: October
       House, 1970.
   1273. Night-blooming cereus. Detroit: Broadside, and Lon-
       don: Breman, 1972.

HAYES, Alfred
   1274. Welcome to the castle. New York: Harper, 1950.
   1275. Just before the divorce. New York: Atheneum, 1968.

HAYS, H. R.
   1276. Selected poems. San Francisco: Kayak, 1968.

HAZEL, Robert
   1277. American elegies. Grand Forks: University of North
       Dakota Press, 1968.

HAZO, Samuel
   1278. Discovery. New York: Sheed and Ward, 1959.
   1279. The quiet wars. New York: Sheed and Ward, 1962.
   1280. Listen with the eye. Pittsburgh: University of Pitts-
       burgh Press, 1964.
   1281. My sons in God. Pittsburgh: University of Pittsburgh
       Press, 1965.
   1282. Blood rights. Pittsburgh: University of Pittsburgh
       Press, 1968.
   1283. Twelve poems. Pittsburgh, 1970.
   1284. Once for the last bandit. Pittsburgh: University of
       Pittsburgh Press, 1972.

HECHT, Anthony
  1285. A summoning of stones. New York: Macmillan, 1954.
  1286. The seven deadly sins. Northampton, MA: Gehenna,
     1958.
  1287. The hard hours. New York: Atheneum, 1967.

HECHT, Roger
  1288. 27 poems. Denver: Swallow, 1966.
  1289. Signposts. Chicago: Swallow, 1970.

HEDLEY, Leslie Woolf
  1290. Death of a world. San Francisco: Inferno, 1951.
  1291. Selected poems, 1946-1953. Sausalito, CA: Golden
     Goose, 1953.
  1292. Abraxas. San Francisco: Inferno, 1960.

HELLER, Michael
  1293. Accidental center. Fremont, MI: Sumac, 1972.

HEMINWAY, David Mason
  1294. Guitar in tissue paper. Baltimore: Contemporary
     Poetry, 1964.
  1295. Where the bone is green. Baltimore: Contemporary
     Poetry, 1969.

HEMSCHEMEYER, Judith
  1296. I remember the room was filled with light. Middle-
     town, CT: Wesleyan University Press, 1973.

HENDERSON, David
  1297. Felix of the silent forest. New York: Poets Press,
     1967.
  1298. De mayor of Harlem. New York: Dutton, 1970.

HEROLD, Brenda
  1299. The St. Charles gig. New York: Corinth, 1971.

HERSCHBERGER, Ruth Margaret
  1300. A way of happening. New York: Pellegrini and Cudahy,
     1948.
  1301. Nature and love poems. New York: Eakins, 1969.

HERSHON, Robert
  1302. Swans loving bears burning the melting deer. Trumans-
     burg, NY: New/Books, 1967.
  1303. Atlantic Avenue. Santa Barbara: Unicorn, 1970.
  1304. Grocery lists. Trumansburg, NY: Crossing Press,
     1972.
  1305. Little red wagon painted blue. Greensboro, NC: Uni-
     corn, 1973.

HEWITT, Geof
  1306. Poem and other poems. Montclair, NJ: Kumquat, 1966.

1307.   Waking up still pickled.   Aurora, NY: Lillabulero,
        1967.

HEYEN, William
1308.   Depth of field.   Baton Rouge: Louisiana State Univer-
        sity Press, 1970.

HIATT, Ben L.
1309.   A solitary tribute to the hermit of Bald Mountain.
        Sacramento: Runcible Spoon, n. d.
1310.   Seattle potlatch.   Sacramento: Island City Press, 1967.
1311.   Fish poems.   Sacramento: Runcible Spoon, 1968.
1312.   A new route.   Sacramento: Runcible Spoon, 1968.

HIGGINS, Dick
1313.   Jefferson's birthday and postface.   New York: Some-
        thing Else, 1964.
1314.   A book about love & war & death.   San Francisco:
        Nova Broadcast, 1969.

HILL, Tom
1315.   Whales.   San Francisco: Twowindows, 1973.

HILLBERRY, Conrad
1316.   Encounter on Burrows Hill.   Athens: Ohio University
        Press, 1969.

HILTON, David
1317.   Moving day.   Madison, WI: Abraxas, 1969.

HINE, Daryl
1318.   Five poems.   Toronto: Emblem Books, 1955.
1319.   The carnal and the crane.   Montreal: Contact, 1957.
1320.   The devil's picture book.   London, New York: Abelard-
        Schuman, 1961.
1321.   The wooden horse.   New York: Atheneum, 1965.
1322.   Minutes.   New York: Atheneum, 1968.

HIRSCHMAN, Jack
1323.   Fragments.   New York: privately printed, 1952.
1324.   A correspondence of Americans.   Bloomington: Indiana
        University Press, 1960.
1325.   Interchange.   Los Angeles: Zora Gallery, 1963.
1326.   Two.   Los Angeles: Zora Gallery, 1963.
1327.   Kline sky.   Northridge, CA: privately printed, 1965.
1328.   YOD.   London: Trigram, 1966.
1329.   London seen directly.   London: Cape Goliard, 1967.
1330.   Wasn't it like this in the woodcut?   London: Cape
        Goliard, 1967.
1331.   William Blake.   Topanga, CA: Love Press, 1967.
1332.   Black alephs: complete lyrics of 1960-68.   London:
        Trigram, 1969.
1333.   Shekinah.   Mill Valley, CA: Maya, 1969.

1334.   The burning of Los Angeles.   Berkeley: J'ose, 1971.
1335.   Scintilla.   Bolinas, CA: Tree Books, 1971.
1336.   Adamnan.   Santa Barbara: Christopher's Press, 1972.

HITCHCOCK, George
1337.   Poems and prints.   San Francisco: San Francisco Review, 1962.
1338.   Tactics of survival.   San Francisco: Bindweed, 1964.
1339.   The dolphin with the revolver in its teeth.   Santa Barbara: Unicorn, 1967.
1340.   A ship of bells.   San Francisco: Kayak, 1968.
1341.   Ten stanzas in praise of the holy chariot.   San Francisco: Kayak, 1969.
1342.   The rococo eye.   La Crosse, WI: Juniper, 1970.
1343.   Another shore.   Santa Cruz, CA: Kayak, 1972.

HOAGLAND, Everett
1344.   Ten poems.   Lincoln University, PA: American Studies Institute, 1969.
1345.   Black velvet.   Detroit: Broadside, 1970.

HOCHMAN, Sandra
1346.   Voyage home.   Paris: Two Cities, 1960.
1347.   Manhattan pastures.   New Haven: Yale University Press, 1963.
1348.   The vaudeville marriage.   New York: Viking, 1966.
1349.   Love letters from Asia.   New York: Viking, 1968.
1350.   Earthworks; poems, 1960-1970.   New York: Viking, 1970.

HODGES, Frenchy Jolene
1351.   Black wisdom.   Detroit: Broadside, 1971.

HOFFMAN, Daniel G.
1352.   An armada of thirty whales.   New Haven: Yale University Press, 1954.
1353.   The city of satisfactions.   New York and London: Oxford University Press, 1963.
1354.   A little geste.   New York and London: Oxford University Press, 1960.
1355.   Striking the stones.   New York and London: Oxford University Press, 1968.
1356.   Broken laws.   New York and London: Oxford University Press, 1970.

HOFFMAN, Jill
1357.   Mink coat.   New York: Holt, Rinehart and Winston, 1973.

HOLDEN, Jonathan
1358.   Design for a house.   Columbia: University of Missouri Press, 1972.

HOLLANDER, John
1359.   A crackling of thorns.   New Haven: Yale University
        Press, 1958.
1360.   Movie-going.   New York: Atheneum, 1962.
1361.   Visions from the Ramble.   New York: Atheneum, 1965.
1362.   Philomel.   London: Turret Books, 1968.
1363.   Types of shape.   New York: Atheneum, 1969.
1364.   The night mirror.   New York: Atheneum, 1971.
1365.   Town and country matters.   Boston: Godine, 1973.

HOLMES, John
1366.   Fair warning.   New York: Holt, 1939.
1367.   Map of my country.   New York: Duell, 1943.
1368.   Address to the living.   New York: Twayne, 1949.
1369.   The double root.   New York: Twayne, 1950.
1370.   The symbols.   Iowa City: Prairie Press, 1955.
1371.   The fortune teller.   New York: Harper, 1961.
1372.   Selected poems.   Boston: Beacon, 1965.

HOLMES, Theodore
1373.   The harvest and the scythe.   New York: Scribner,
        1957.
1374.   Ship on the beach.   London: Fortune, 1965.
1375.   An upland pasture.   Nashville: Vanderbilt University
        Press, 1966.

HOMPSON, Davi Det
1376.   Oh, no.   Norwood, PA: Telegraph Books, 1972.

HONIG, Edwin
1377.   The moral circus.   Baltimore: Contemporary Poetry,
        1955.
1378.   The gazabos: 41 poems.   New York: Clarke and Way,
        1959.
1379.   Survivals.   New York: October House, 1964.
1380.   Spring journal.   Middletown, CT: Wesleyan University
        Press, 1968.
1381.   Calisto and Melibea.   Providence, RI: Hellcoal, 1972.
1382.   Four springs.   Chicago: Swallow, 1972.

HOOKER, Craig M.
1383.   For we are all gifted and real.   Berkeley: Oyez, 1972.

HORGAN, Paul
1384.   Songs after Lincoln.   New York: Farrar, Straus,
        1965.

HORNE, Frank
1385.   Haverstraw.   London: Breman, 1963.

HORSLEY, James
1386.   God's naked daughter.   Berkeley: Oyez, 1972.

HOSKINS, Katherine
   1387. A penitential primer. Cummington, MA: Cummington, 1945.
   1388. Villa Narcisse: the garden, the statues, and the pool. New York: Noonday, 1956.
   1389. Out in the open. New York: Macmillan, 1959.
   1390. Excursions. New York: Atheneum, 1967.

HOTTELL, Christopher
   1391. The knives of dawn. Berkeley: Oyez, 1970.

HOUSTON, Peyton
   1392. Sonnet variations. Highlands, NC: J. Williams, 1962.
   1393. For the remarkable animals. Providence, RI: Burning Deck, 1970.

HOWARD, Richard
   1394. Quantities. Middletown, CT: Wesleyan University Press, 1962.
   1395. The damages. Middletown, CT: Wesleyan University Press, 1967.
   1396. Untitled subjects. New York: Atheneum, 1969.
   1397. Findings. New York: Atheneum, 1971.
   1398. Preferences. New York: Viking, 1973.

HOWARD, Vanessa
   1399. A screaming whisper. New York: Holt, Rinehart and Winston, 1972.

HOWE, Fanny
   1400. Eggs. Boston: Houghton Mifflin, 1970.

HOWES, Barbara
   1401. The undersea farmer. Pawlet, VT: Banyan, 1948.
   1402. In the cold country. New York: Grove, 1954.
   1403. Light and dark. Middletown, CT: Wesleyan University Press, 1959.
   1404. Looking up at leaves. New York: Knopf, 1966.
   1405. The blue garden. Middletown, CT: Wesleyan University Press, 1972.

HOWES, Victor
   1406. Lobsterman's daughter. Boston: Northeastern University Press, 1969.

HOYEM, Andrew
   1407. The wake. San Francisco: Auerhahn, 1963.
   1408. The music room. San Francisco: Haselwood, 1965.
   1409. Articles. New York: Grossman, 1969.

HUBBELL, Lindley William
   1410. Dark pavilion. New Haven: Yale University Press, 1927.

57   Huckaby

1411. Seventy poems. Denver: Swallow, 1965.
1412. Atlantic triptych. Kobe, Japan: Ikuta, 1971.
1413. Autobiography. Kobe, Japan: Ikuta, 1971.

HUCKABY, Gerald
1414. City, uncity. Garden City, NY: Doubleday, 1969.

HUFF, Robert
1415. Colonel Johnson's ride. Detroit: Wayne State Univer-
       sity Press, 1959.
1416. The course: one, two, three, now! Detroit: Wayne
       State University Press, 1966.
1417. The ventriloquist. Chicago: Swallow, 1973.

HUGHES, Daniel
1418. Walking in a tree. New York: October House, 1964.

HUGHES, Dorothy Berry
1419. The green loving. New York: Scribner, 1953.
1420. The great victory mosaic. Columbia: University of
       Missouri Press, 1971.

HUGHES, Langston
1421. The weary blues. New York: Knopf, 1926.
1422. Fine clothes to the Jew. New York: Knopf, 1927.
1423. Dear lovely death. Amenia, NY: privately printed,
       Troutbeck, 1931.
1424. The negro mother. New York: Golden Stair, 1931.
1425. The dream keeper. New York: Knopf, 1932.
1426. Scottsboro limited. New York: Golden Stair, 1932.
1427. A new song. New York: International Workers Order,
       1938.
1428. Shakespeare in Harlem. New York: Knopf, 1942.
1429. Freedom's plow. NY: Musette, 1943.
1430. Jim Crow's last stand. New York: Negro Publication
       Society of America, 1943.
1431. Lament for dark peoples. New York: Holt, and Am-
       sterdam: H. van Krimpen, 1944.
1432. Fields of wonder. New York: Knopf, 1947.
1433. One-way ticket. New York: Knopf, 1949.
1434. Montage of a dream deferred. New York: Holt, 1951.
1435. Selected poems. New York: Knopf, 1959.
1436. Ask your mama: 12 moods for jazz. New York:
       Knopf, 1961.
1437. The panther & the lash; poems of our times. New
       York: Knopf, 1967.
1438. Don't you turn back. New York: Knopf, 1969.

HUGO, Richard
1439. A run of jacks. Minneapolis: University of Minnesota
       Press, 1961.
1440. Death of the Kapowsin tavern. New York: Harcourt,
       Brace, 1965.

1441. Good luck in cracked Italian. New York: World, 1969.
1442. The lady in kicking horse reservoir. New York:
       Norton, 1973.

HULL, William
1443. Selected poems, 1942-1952. New York: Brigant, 1954.
1444. Dandy Brown. Denver: Experiment, 1959.
1445. The other side of silence. New York: Swallowtree,
       1964.
1446. Collected poems, 1942-1968. Calcutta: Writers Work-
       shop, and Merrick, NY: Lee Smith, 1969.

HUME, Martha Haskins
1447. Sutras and shadows. Denver: Swallow, 1965.

HUMPHREY, James
1448. Argument for love. Falmouth, MA: Kendall, 1970.

HUMPHRIES, Rolfe
1449. Poems. New York: Scribner, 1954.
1450. Green armor on green ground; poems in the twenty-
       four official Welsh meters and some, in free meters,
       on Welsh themes. New York: Scribner, 1956.
1451. Collected poems. Bloomington: Indiana University
       Press, 1965.
1452. Coat on a stick. Bloomington: University of Indiana
       Press, 1969.

HUNT, William
1453. Of the map that changes. Chicago: Swallow, 1973.

HUNTER, Kristin
1454. Boss cat. New York: Scribner, 1971.

HUNTING, Constance
1455. The heron. West Lafayette. IN: F. Stefanile, 1963.
1456. After the Stravinsky concert. New York: Scribner,
       1969.
1457. Cimmerian and other poems. Orono, ME: Pucker-
       brush, 1972.

IFETAYO, Femi Funmi (Regina Micou)
1458. We the Black woman. Detroit: Broadside, 1970.

IGNATOW, David
1459. Poems. Prairie City, IL: Decker, 1948.
1460. The gentle weight lifter. New York: Morris Gallery,
       1955.
1461. Say pardon. Middletown, CT: Wesleyan University
       Press, 1961.
1462. Figures of the human. Middletown, CT: Wesleyan

University Press, 1964.
1463. Earth hard: selected poems. London: Rapp and Whit-
       ing, 1968.
1464. Rescue the dead. Middletown, CT: Wesleyan Univer-
       sity Press, 1968.
1465. Poems, 1934-1969. Middletown, CT: Wesleyan Univer-
       sity Press, 1970.

INADA, Lawson Fusao
1466. Before the war; poems as they happened. New York:
       Morrow, 1971.

INEZ, Colette
1467. The woman who loved worms. Garden City, NY:
       Doubleday, 1972.

INGALLS, Jeremy
1468. The woman from the island. Chicago: H. Regnery,
       1958.
1469. These islands also. Rutland, VT: Tuttle, 1959.

IRBY, Kenneth
1470. Relation; poems, 1965-1966. Los Angeles: Black
       Sparrow, 1970.

JACKMON, Marvin see X, Marvin

JACOBSEN, Josephine
1471. For the unlost. Baltimore: Contemporary Poetry,
       1946.
1472. The human climate, new poems. Baltimore: Contem-
       porary Poetry, 1953.
1473. The animal inside. Athens: Ohio University Press,
       1966.

JAMES, Thomas
1474. Letters to a stranger. Boston: Houghton Mifflin, 1973.

JARRELL, Randall
1475. The rage for the lost penny. New York: New Direc-
       tions, 1940.
1476. Blood for a stranger. New York: Harcourt, Brace,
       1942.
1477. Little friend, little friend. New York: Dial, 1945.
1478. Losses. New York: Harcourt, Brace, 1948.
1479. The seven-league crutches. New York: Harcourt,
       Brace, 1951.
1480. Selected poems. New York: Knopf, 1955.
1481. The woman at the Washington Zoo; poems and transla-
       tions. New York: Atheneum, 1960.
1482. Selected poems, including The woman at the Washington

Zoo. New York: Atheneum, 1964.
1483.   The lost world. New York: Macmillan, 1965; London:
Eyre & Spottiswoode, 1966.
1484.   The complete poems. New York: Farrar, Straus,
1969; London: Faber, 1971.

JARRETT, Emmett
1485.   The days. Cambridge, MA: Bean Bag, 1968.
1486.   Greek fleet. Trumansburg, NY: Crossing Press, 1972.

JEFFERS, Lance
1487.   My blackness is the beauty of this land. Detroit:
Broadside, 1970.
1488.   Man with a furnace in his hand. Detroit: Broadside,
1971.

JENNINGS, Henry see WOLDE, Habte

JEROME, Judson
1489.   Light in the west. Francestown, NH: Golden Quill,
1962.
1490.   The ocean's warning to the skin diver and other love
poems. Point Richmond, CA: Crown Point, 1964.
1491.   Serenade. Point Richmond, CA: Crown Point, 1968.

JOANS, Ted
1492.   All of Ted Joans and no more. New York: Excelsior,
1961.
1493.   Black pow-wow: jazz poems. New York: Hill &
Wang, 1969; London: Calder & Boyars, 1973.
1494.   Afrodisia. New York: Hill & Wang, 1971.

JOHN, George William
1495.   A garland about me. Baltimore: Contemporary Poetry,
1951.
1496.   If madness were bred. Baltimore: Contemporary Poe-
try, 1956.

JOHNSON, Carol
1497.   Figure for Scamander. Denver: Swallow, 1964.

JOHNSON, Denis
1498.   The man among the seals. Iowa City: Stone Wall,
1970.

JOHNSON, Halvard
1499.   Transparencies and projections. New York: New
Rivers, 1969.
1500.   The dance of the red swan. New York: New Rivers,
1971.

JOHNSON, Ronald
1501.   A line of poetry, a row of trees. Highlands, NC:

J. Williams, 1964.
1502. Assorted jungles: Rousseau. San Francisco: Auer-
     hahn, 1966.
1503. Gorse/Goose/Rose. Bloomington: Indiana University
     Fine Arts Department, 1966.
1504. The book of the green man. New York: Norton, and
     London: Longmans Green, 1967.
1505. Balloons for moonless nights. Urbana, IL: Finial,
     1968.
1506. Valley of the many-colored grasses. New York: Nor-
     ton, 1969.

JONES, Donald
1507. Medical aid. Lincoln: University of Nebraska Press,
     1967.
1508. Miss Liberty, meet Crazy Horse. Chicago: Swallow,
     1972.

JONES, Jeanetta
1509. How to invoke a garden, how to invoke the same garden.
     Berkeley: Sand Dollar, 1971.

JONES, LeRoi (Imamu Amiri Baraka)
1510. Preface to a twenty volume suicide note. New York:
     Totem/Corinth Books, 1961.
1511. The dead lecturer. New York: Grove, 1964.
1512. Black art. Newark, NJ: Jihad, 1969.
1513. Black magic; poetry 1961-1967. Indianapolis: Bobbs-
     Merrill, 1969.
1514. It's nation time. Chicago: Third World, 1970.

JONG, Erica
1515. Fruits & vegetables. New York: Holt, Rinehart and
     Winston, 1971; London: Secker & Warburg, 1973.
1516. Half-lives. New York: Holt, Rinehart and Winston,
     1973.

JORDAN, June
1517. Who look at me. New York: Crowell, 1969.
1518. Destination: fishes. Chicago: Third World, 1971.
1519. [no entry]
1520. Some changes. New York: Dutton, 1971.
1521. [no entry]

JUDSON, John
1522. Finding words in winter. New Rochelle, NY: Eliza-
     beth, 1973.

JUNKINS, Donald
1523. The sunfish and the partridge. Cambridge, MA: Pym-
     Randall, 1965.
1524. And sandpipers she said. Amherst: University of
     Massachusetts Press, 1970.

JUSTICE, Donald
  1525. Beyond the hunting woods. Ann Arbor: University
          Microfilms, 1954.
  1526. The summer anniversaries. Middletown, CT: Wesleyan
          University Press, 1960.
  1527. A local storm. Iowa City: Stone Wall, 1963.
  1528. Night light. Middletown, CT: Wesleyan University
          Press, 1967.
  1529. Departures. New York: Atheneum, 1973.

KALI see GROSVENOR, Kali

KALLMAN, Chester
  1530. Storm at Castelfranco. New York: Grove, 1956.
  1531. Absent and present. Middletown, CT: Wesleyan University Press, 1963.
  1532. The sense of occasion. New York: Braziller, 1971.

KAMINSKY, Marc
  1533. Birthday poems. New York: Horizon, 1972.

KAMINSKY, Peretz
  1534. Reflection in the eye of God. New York: Blom, 1969.
  1535. Adam, Cain and other prayers. New York: Blom, 1970.
  1536. The book of rituals. New York: Horizon, 1971.
  1537. The book of questions. New York: Horizon, 1972.

KANDEL, Lenore
  1538. A passing dragon--a passing dragon seen again--the exquisite navel. Los Angeles: Three Penny, 1959.
  1539. The love book. San Francisco: Stolen Paper, 1966.
  1540. Word alchemy. New York: Grove, 1967.

KAPLAN, Allan
  1541. Paper airplane. New York: Harper & Row, 1971.

KAPLAN, Bernard
  1542. Prisoners of this world. New York: Grossman, 1970.

KAPLAN, Milton
  1543. In a time between wars. New York: Norton, 1973.

KATZ, Menke
  1544. Twelve poems of Menke Katz. Brooklyn: privately printed, 1964.
  1545. Land of manna. Chicago: Windfall, 1965.
  1546. Rockrose. New York: Smith-Horizon, 1970.
  1547. Burning village. New York: Horizon, 1973.

63 Katz

KATZ, Steve
1548. Cheyenne river wild track. Ithaca, NY: Ithaca House, 1973.

KATZMAN, Allen
1549. The immaculate. Garden City, NY: Doubleday, 1970.

KAUFMAN, Bob
1550. Abomunist manifesto. San Francisco: City Lights, 1959.
1551. Second April. San Francisco: City Lights, 1959.
1552. Solitudes crowded with loneliness. New York: New Directions, 1965.
1553. Golden sardine. San Francisco: City Lights, 1967.

KAUFMAN, Shirley
1554. The floor keeps turning. Pittsburgh: University of Pittsburgh Press, 1970.
1555. Gold country. Pittsburgh: University of Pittsburgh Press, 1973.

KAY, Ellen
1556. A local habitation. Denver: Swallow, 1958.

KEES, Weldon
1557. The last man. San Francisco: Colt, 1943.
1558. The fall of the magicians. New York: Reynal, 1947.
1559. Poems, 1947-1954. San Francisco: A. Wilson, 1954.
1560. Collected poems. Iowa City: Stone Wall, 1960.

KEITHLEY, George
1561. The Donner party. New York: Braziller, 1972.

KELLY, Dave
1562. All here together. Ithaca, NY: Lillabulero, 1969.
1563. Dear Nate. Sacramento: Runcible Spoon, 1969.
1564. Summer study. Sacramento: Runcible Spoon, 1969.
1565. Instructions for viewing a solar eclipse. Middletown, CT: Wesleyan University Press, 1972.
1566. At a time: a dance for voices. Fredonia, NY: Basilisk, 1973.

KELLY, Robert
1567. Armed descent. New York: Hawks Well, 1961.
1568. Her body against time. Mexico City: El Corno Emplumado, 1962.
1569. Round dances. Privately printed, 1964.
1570. Lectiones. Placitas, NM: Duende, 1965.
1571. Lunes. New York: Hawks Well, 1965.
1572. Weeks. Mexico City: El Corno Emplumado, 1966.
1573. Axon dendron tree. Annandale-on-Hudson, NY: Salitter, 1967.
1574. Devotions. Annandale-on-Hudson, NY: Salitter, 1967.

1575. A joining: a sequence for H. D. San Francisco: Black Sparrow, 1967.
1576. Twenty poems. Privately printed, 1967.
1577. Finding the measure. Los Angeles: Black Sparrow, 1968.
1578. Songs I-**XXX**. Cambridge, MA: Pym-Randall, 1968.
1579. Sonnets, 1967. Los Angeles: Black Sparrow, 1968.
1580. The common shore, books I-V; a long poem about America in time. Los Angeles: Black Sparrow, 1969.
1581. Kali yuga. London: Cape Goliard, 1970.
1582. Cities. West Newbury, MA: Frontier, 1971.
1583. Flesh, dream, book. Los Angeles: Black Sparrow, 1971.
1584. In time. West Newbury, MA: Frontier, 1971.
1585. The mill particulars. Los Angeles: Black Sparrow, 1973.

KENDALL, Lace (see also STOUTENBURG, Adrien)
1585a. Heroes, advise us. New York: Scribner, 1964.

KENNEDY, X. J.
1586. Nude descending a staircase; poems, songs, a ballad. Garden City, NY: Doubleday, 1961.
1587. Growing into love. Garden City, NY: Doubleday, 1969.
1588. Breaking and entering. London: Oxford University Press, 1971.
1589. Emily Dickinson in Southern California. Boston: Godine, 1973.

KENSETH, Arnold
1590. The holy merriment. Chapel Hill: University of North Carolina Press, 1963.

KERN, W. Bliem
1591. Meditationsmeditationsmeditations. New York: New Rivers, 1973.

KEROUAC, Jack
1592. Mexico City blues. New York: Grove, 1959.
1593. The scripture of the golden eternity. New York: Totem, 1960.
1594. Rimbaud. San Francisco: City Lights, 1960.
1595. Scattered poems. San Francisco: City Lights, 1971.

KESSLER, Jascha
1596. Whatever love declares. Los Angeles: Plantin, 1969.
1597. After the armies have passed. New York: New York University Press, 1970.

KESSLER, Milton
1598. A road came once. Columbus: Ohio State University Press, 1963.

1599. Called home. New York: Black Bird, 1967.
1600. Heart stones. Boston: Impressions Workshop, 1970.
1601. Sailing too far. New York: Harper & Row, 1973.

KGOSITSILE, Keorapetse W.
  1602. Spirits unchained. Detroit: Broadside, 1969.
  1603. For Melba. Chicago: Third World, 1970.
  1604. My name is Afrika. Garden City, NY: Doubleday,
      1971.

KIDD, Walter E. see PENDLETON, Conrad

KIESEL, Stanley
  1605. The pearl is a hardened sinner; notes from kinder-
      garten. New York: Scribner, 1968.

KILGORE, James C.
  1606. A time of Black devotion. Ashland, OH: Ashland
      Poetry Press, 1971.

KINNELL, Galway
  1607. What a kingdom it was. Boston: Houghton Mifflin,
      1960.
  1608. Flower herding on Mount Monadnock. Boston: Hough-
      ton Mifflin, 1964.
  1609. Poems of night. London: Rapp & Carroll, 1968.
  1610. Body rags. Boston: Houghton Mifflin, 1968.
  1611. The book of nightmares. Boston: Houghton Mifflin,
      1971.

KIRSTEIN, Lincoln
  1612. Notre Dame des Cadres. New York: Modern Editions,
      1933.
  1613. Low ceiling. New York: Putnam, 1935.
  1614. Rhymes of a Pfc. New York: New Directions, 1964.
  1615. Rhymes and more rhymes of a Pfc. New York: New
      Directions, 1966.

KIZER, Carolyn
  1616. The ungrateful garden. Bloomington: Indiana Univer-
      sity Press, 1961.
  1617. Knock upon silence. Garden City, NY: Doubleday,
      1965.
  1618. Midnight was my cry. Garden City, NY: Doubleday,
      1971.

KLAPPERT, Peter
  1619. Lugging vegetables to Nantucket. New Haven: Yale
      University Press, 1971.

KLEYHAUER, Alfred Deitrich
  1620. Black. Denver: Swallow, 1966.

KLIMO, Jonathan
    1621. The great nebula. Providence, RI: Hellcoal, 1972.

KNIGHT, Etheridge
    1622. Poems from prison. Detroit: Broadside, 1968.
    1623. Belly song. Detroit: Broadside, 1973.

KNOEPFLE, John
    1624. Rivers into islands. Chicago: University of Chicago Press, 1965.
    1625. After gray days. Prairie Village, KA: Crabgrass, 1969.
    1626. Songs for Gail Guidry's guitar. New York: New Rivers, 1969.
    1627. The intricate land. New York: New Rivers, 1970.

KNOTT, Bill
    1628. The naomi poems book one: corpse and beans. Chicago: Follett, 1968.
    1629. Auto-necrophilia. Chicago: Desnos Books, 1969.
    1630. Auto-necrophilia; the _____ poems, book 2. Chicago: Big Table, 1971.
    1631. Love poems to myself. Boston: Barn Dream, 1973.

KOCH, Kenneth
    1632. Poems. New York: Tibor de Nagy, 1953.
    1633. Ko; or, A season on earth. New York: Grove, 1960.
    1634. Permanently. New York: Tiber, 1960.
    1635. Thank you. New York: Grove, 1962.
    1636. Poems, from 1952 and 1953. Los Angeles: Black Sparrow, 1968.
    1637. The pleasures of peace. New York: Grove, 1969.
    1638. Sleeping with women. Los Angeles: Black Sparrow, 1969.
    1639. When the sun tries to go on. Los Angeles: Black Sparrow, 1969.

KOEHLER, Stanley
    1640. The fact of fall. Amherst: University of Massachusetts Press, 1969.

KOERTGE, Ronald
    1641. The father-poems. Fremont, MI: Sumac, 1973.

KOETHE, John
    1642. Domes. New York: Columbia University Press, 1973.

KOLLER, James
    1643. Brainard and Washington Street poems. Eugene, OR: Toad, 1965.
    1644. Two hands; poems, 1959-1961. Seattle: James B. Smith, 1965.
    1645. The dogs of other dark woods. San Francisco: Four

Seasons, 1966.
1646. Some cows; poems of civilization and domestic life.
San Francisco: Coyote Books, 1966.
1647. I went to see my true love. Buffalo, NY: Audit East/
West, 1967.
1648. California poems. Los Angeles: Black Sparrow, 1971.

KOOSER, Ted
1649. Official entry blank. Lincoln: University of Nebraska
Press, 1969.
1650. Grass county. Lincoln, NE: Windflower, 1971.
1651. How to. Crete, NE: Best Cellar, 1973.

KÖRTE, Mary Norbert
1652. Hymn to the gentle sun. Berkeley: Oyez, 1967.
1653. Beginning of lines; response to Albion Moonlight.
Berkeley: Oyez, 1968.
1654. The generation of love. New York: Bruce, 1969.
1655. The midnight bridge. Berkeley: Oyez, 1970.

KRAMER, Aaron
1656. The tune of the calliope. New York: T. Yoseloff,
1958.
1657. Moses; poems and translations. New York: O'Hare,
1962.
1658. Rumshinsky's hat and House of buttons; two collections
of poetry. New York: T. Yoseloff, 1964.
1659. On the way to Palermo. New York: A. S. Barnes;
and London: T. Yoseloff, 1973.

KRANES, David
1660. Margins. New York: Knopf, 1972.

KRAUSS, Ruth
1661. The cantilever rainbow. New York: Pantheon Books,
1965.
1662. There's a little ambiguity over there among the blue-
bells, and other theater poems. New York: Some-
thing Else, 1968.
1663. Somebody else's nut tree. Lenox, MA: Lenox Book-
store, 1971.
1664. This breast gothic. Lenox, MA: Lenox Bookstore,
1973.

KRECH, Richard
1665. How easily your mind can slip off. Sacramento: Run-
cible Spoon, 1967.
1666. We are on the verge of ecstasy. Cleveland: 7 Flowers,
1967.
1667. The hashish scarab. Sacramento: Runcible Spoon, 1968.

KRICKEL, Edward
1668. Segment of a view. Memphis: Argus Books, 1965.

KROLL, Ernest
1669. Cape Horn. New York: Dutton, 1952.
1670. The pauses of the eye. New York: Dutton, 1955.

KROLL, Judith
1671. In the temperate zone. New York: Scribner, 1973.

KUMIN, Maxine
1672. Halfway. New York: Holt, Rinehart and Winston, 1961.
1673. The privilege. New York: Harper & Row, 1965.
1674. The nightmare factory. New York: Harper & Row, 1970.
1675. Up country; poems of New England, new and selected. New York: Harper & Row, 1972.

KUNITZ, Stanley
1676. Intellectual things. Garden City, NY: Doubleday, 1930.
1677. Passport to the war. Holt, Rinehart and Winston, 1944.
1678. Selected poems, 1928-1958. Boston: Little, Brown, 1958; London: J. M. Dent, 1959.
1679. The testing-tree. Boston: Little, Brown, 1971.

KUTZIN, Alice
1680. The blind date that made it. New York: McKay, 1971.

KUZMA, Greg
1681. Sitting around. Northwood Narrows, NH: Lillabulero, 1969.
1682. Something at last visible. East Lansing, MI: Zeitgeist, 1969.
1683. The Bosporus. Belmont, MA: Hellric, 1971.
1684. Harry's things. Springfield, IL: Apple, 1971.
1685. Song for someone going away. Ithaca, NY: Ithaca House, 1971.
1686. Good news. New York: Viking, 1973.
1687. A problem of high water. Reno: West Coast Poetry Review, 1973.
1688. What friends are for. Crete, NE: Best Cellar, 1973.

KYGER, Joanne
1689. The tapestry and the web. San Francisco: Four Seasons, 1965.
1690. Joanne. New York: Angel Hair, 1970.
1691. Places to go. Los Angeles: Black Sparrow, 1971.

LaBELLE, Christine
1692. The possibility of an early fall. New Rochelle, NY: Elizabeth, 1971.

LAING, Dilys
- 1693. Walk through two landscapes. New York: Twayne, 1949.
- 1694. Poems from a cage; new, selected, and translated poems. New York: Macmillan, 1961.
- 1695. The collected poems of Dilys Laing. Cleveland: Case Western Reserve University Press, 1967.

LAMANTIA, Philip
- 1696. Erotic Poems. Berkeley: Bern Porter, 1946.
- 1697. Ekstasis. San Francisco: Auerhahn, 1959.
- 1698. Narcotica. San Francisco: Auerhahn, 1959.
- 1699. Destroyed works. San Francisco: Auerhahn, 1962.
- 1700. Touch of the marvelous. Berkeley: Oyez, 1966.
- 1701. Selected poems, 1943-1966. San Francisco: City Lights, 1967.
- 1702. The blood of the air. San Francisco: Four Seasons, 1970.

LANGLAND, Joseph
- 1703. For Harold. Augsburg, Germany, 1945.
- 1704. The green town. New York: Scribner, 1956.
- 1705. A little homily. Northampton, MA: Apiary, 1962.
- 1706. The wheel of summer. New York: Dial, 1963.
- 1707. Adlai Stevenson. Iowa City: Stone Wall, 1970.

LANSING, Gerrit
- 1708. The heavenly tree grows downward. Annandale-on-Hudson, NY: Matter Books, 1966.
- 1709. Working in the lower red field. Cambridge, MA, 1969.

LARSSON, Raymond Edward Francis
- 1710. Weep and prepare. New York: Coward, 1940.
- 1711. Book like a bow curved. Detroit: University of Detroit Press, 1961.

LATIMORE, Jewel C. see AMINI, Johari

LATTIMORE, Richmond
- 1712. Poems. Ann Arbor: University of Michigan Press, 1957.
- 1713. Sestina for a far-off summer; poems, 1957-1962. Ann Arbor: University of Michigan Press, 1962.
- 1714. The stride of time; new poems and translations. Ann Arbor: University of Michigan Press, 1966.
- 1715. Poems from three decades. New York: Scribner, 1972.

LAUGHLIN, James
- 1716. Some natural things. New York: New Directions, 1945.
- 1717. Report on a visit to Germany. Lausanne: Held, 1948.
- 1718. A small book of poems. Milan: Scheiwiller, and New York: New Directions, 1948.

1719. The wild anemone. Verona: Valdonega, and New York: New Directions, 1957.
1720. Confidential report. London: Gaberbocchus, 1959.
1721. Selected poems. Norfolk, CT: New Directions, 1959.
1722. The pig. Mt. Horeb, WI: Perishable Press, 1970.

LAWLESS, Ken
1723. Tailing off. East Lansing, MI: Zeitgeist, 1969.
1724. Amper-sand & question-mark; a finite poem. East Lansing, MI: Zeitgeist, 1970.
1725. Twenty characters in search of an academic novel. East Lansing, MI: Zeitgeist, 1970.

LAWNER, Lynne
1726. Wedding night of a nun. Boston: Little, Brown, 1964.
1727. Triangle dream. New York: Harper & Row, 1969.

LAWSON, Todd
1728. Patriotic poems of Amerikkka. San Francisco: Peace & Pieces, 1971.

LAX, Robert
1729. The circus of the sun. New York: Journeyman Books, 1959.
1730. New poems. New York: Journeyman Books, 1962.
1731. Sea poem. Scotland: Wild Hawthorne, 1966.
1732. Thought. New York: Journeyman Books, 1966.
1733. 3 or 4 poems about the sea. New York: Journeyman Books, 1966.
1734. Black and white. New York: Journeyman Books, 1972.

LAZARD, Naomi
1735. Cry of the peacocks. New York: Harcourt, Brace, 1967.

LAZARUS, A. L.
1736. Entertainments / & valedictions. Iowa City: Windfall, 1970.

LEARY, Paris
1737. Views of the Oxford colleges. New York: Scribner, 1960.

LEE, Don L.
1738. Think black. Chicago: New Act, 1967; Detroit: Broadside, 1968, enl. 1969.
1739. Black pride. Detroit: Broadside, 1968.
1740. Don't cry; scream. Detroit: Broadside, 1969.
1741. We walk the way of the new world. Detroit: Broadside, 1970.
1742. Directionscore: selected and new poems. Detroit: Broadside, 1971.
1743. From planet to planet. Detroit: Broadside, 1973.

LEGLER, Philip
1744.   A change of view.   Lincoln: University of Nebraska
      Press, 1964.
1745.   The intruder.   Athens: University of Georgia Press,
      1972.

L'ENGLE, Madeleine
1746.   Lines scribbled on an envelope.   New York: Farrar,
      Straus, 1969.

LERMAN, Eleanor
1747.   Armed love.   Middletown, CT: Wesleyan University
      Press, 1973.

LEVENDOSKY, Charles
1748.   Perimeters.   Middletown, CT: Wesleyan University
      Press, 1970.

LEVENSON, Christopher
1749.   Stills.   Middletown, CT: Wesleyan University Press,
      1973.

LEVERTOV, Denise
1750.   The double image.   London: Cresset, 1946.
1751.   Here and now.   San Francisco: City Lights, 1957.
1752.   Overland to the islands.   Highlands, NC: Jargon, 1958.
1753.   With eyes at the back of our heads.   New York: New
      Directions, 1960.
1754.   The Jacob's ladder.   New York: New Directions, 1962;
      London: Jonathan Cape, 1965.
1755.   O taste and see.   New York: New Directions, 1964.
1756.   The sorrow dance.   New York: New Directions, 1967;
      London: Jonathan Cape, 1968.
1757.   A tree telling of Orpheus.   Los Angeles: Black Spar-
      row, 1968.
1758.   Embroideries.   Los Angeles: Black Sparrow, 1969.
1759.   Relearning the alphabet.   New York: New Directions,
      1970.
1760.   To stay alive.   New York: New Directions, 1971.
1761.   Footprints.   New York: New Directions, 1972.

LEVINE, Al
1762.   Prophecy in Bridgeport, and other poems.   New York:
      Scribner, 1972.

LEVINE, Philip
1763.   On the edge.   Iowa City: Stone Wall, 1961.
1764.   Not this pig.   Middletown, CT: Wesleyan University
      Press, 1968.
1765.   5 Detroits.   Santa Barbara: Unicorn, 1970.
1766.   Thistles.   London: Turret, 1970.
1767.   Pili's wall.   Santa Barbara: Unicorn, 1971.
1768.   Red dust.   San Francisco: Kayak, 1971.

1769. They feed they lion. New York: Atheneum, 1972.

LEVIS, Larry
      1770. Wrecking crew. Pittsburgh: University of Pittsburgh
             Press, 1972.

LEVY, Lyn
      1771. Singing happy sad. Detroit: Broadside, 1973.

L'HEUREUX, John
      1772. Quick as dandelions. Garden City, NY: Doubleday,
             1964.
      1773. Rubrics for a revolution. New York: Macmillan, 1967.
      1774. One eye and a measuring rod. New York: Macmillan,
             1968.
      1775. No place for hiding; new poems. Garden City, NY:
             Doubleday, 1971.

LIEBERMAN, Laurence
      1776. The unblinding. New York: Macmillan, 1968.
      1777. Osprey suicides. New York: Macmillan, 1973.

LIFSHIN, Lyn
      1778. Leaves and night things. Gorham, ME: Baby John,
             1970.
      1779. Black apples. Trumansburg, NY: Crossing Press,
             1971; enl. 1973.
      1780. With boards & old postcards inside us. Belmont, MA:
             Hellric, 1971.
      1781. Selected poems. Trumansburg, NY: Crossing Press,
             1972.
      1782. Tentacles, leaves. Belmont, MA: Hellric, 1972.
      1783. Museum. Albany, NY: Conspiracy, 1972.

LIMA, Frank
      1784. Underground with the oriole. New York: Dutton, 1971.

LINDQUIST, Ray
      1785. By products. Trumansburg, NY: Crossing Press,
             1972.

LIPSITZ, Lou
      1786. Cold water. Middletown, CT: Wesleyan University
             Press, 1967.

LOCKE, Duane
      1787. From the bottom of the sea. New York: Black Sun,
             1968.
      1788. Inland oceans. Baltimore: Beanbag, 1968.
      1789. Dead cities. Milwaukee: Gunrunner, 1969.
      1790. Rainbows under boards. Tampa, FL: Tampa Poetry
             Review, 1969.
      1791. Light bulbs' lengthened eyelashes and storks' nests.

East Lansing, MI: Ghost Dance, 1970.
1792. The submerged fern in the waistline of solitude. Ann Arbor, MI: Ann Arbor Review, 1972.

LOCKE, Wende
1793. Split hairs. New York: New York University Press, 1970.

LOCKLIN, Gerald
1794. Sunset beach. Torrance, CA: Hors Commerce, 1967.
1795. The toad poems. Sacramento: Runcible Spoon, 1970.

LOEWINSOHN, Ron
1796. Watermelons. New York: Totem, 1959.
1797. The world of the lie. San Francisco: Change, 1963.
1798. Against the silences to come. San Francisco: Four Seasons, 1965.
1799. L'autre. Los Angeles: Black Sparrow, 1967.
1800. Lying together, turning the head and shifting the weight, the produce district and other places, moving--a spring poem. Los Angeles: Black Sparrow, 1967.
1801. The sea, around us. Los Angeles: Black Sparrow, 1968.
1802. The step. Los Angeles: Black Sparrow, 1968.
1803. Meat air: poems, 1957-1969. New York: Harcourt, Brace, 1970.
1804. The leaves. Los Angeles: Black Sparrow, 1973.

LOFTIS, N. J.
1805. Black cinema. New York: Liveright, 1973.

LOGAN, John
1806. Cycle for Mother Cabrini. New York: Grove, 1955.
1807. Ghosts of the heart; new poems. Chicago: University of Chicago Press, 1960.
1808. Spring of the thief; poems, 1960-1962. New York: Knopf, 1963.
1809. The zigzag walk; poems, 1963-1968. New York: Dutton, 1969.
1810. The anonymous lover. New York: Liveright, 1973.

LOMAX, Pearl Cleage
1811. We don't need no music. Detroit: Broadside, 1972.

LONG, Doughtry
1812. Black love, Black hope. Detroit: Broadside, 1971.
1813. Ginger bread mama. Detroit: Broadside, 1971.
1814. Song for Nia; a poetic essay in three parts. Detroit: Broadside, 1971.

LORD, May
1815. On the mown grass. Denver: Swallow, 1961.

LORDE, Audre
    1816. The first cities. New York: Poets Press, 1968.
    1817. Cables to rage. Detroit: Broadside, 1970.
    1818. From a land where other people live. Detroit: Broadside, 1973.

LOURIE, Dick
    1819. The dream telephone. Trumansburg, NY: New/Books, 1968.
    1820. Letter to answer. Greensboro, NC: Unicorn, 1972.
    1821. Stumbling. Trumansburg, NY: Crossing Press, 1973.

LOWELL, Robert
    1822. Land of unlikeness. Cummington, MA: Cummington, 1944.
    1823. Lord Weary's castle. New York: Harcourt, Brace, 1946.
    1824. Poems, 1938-1949. London: Faber, 1950.
    1825. The mills of the Kavanaughs. New York: Harcourt, Brace, 1951.
    1826. Life studies. New York: Farrar, Straus, and London: Faber, 1959.
    1827. Lord Weary's castle, and The mills of the Kavanaughs; two volumes of poems. New York: Meridian Books, 1961.
    1828. Imitations. New York: Noonday, and London: Faber, 1962.
    1829. For the Union dead. New York: Farrar, Straus, 1964; London: Faber, 1965.
    1830. Selected poems. London: Faber, 1965.
    1831. Near the ocean. New York: Farrar, Straus, and London: Faber, 1967.
    1832. The voyage and other versions of poems by Baudelaire. New York: Farrar, Straus, and London: Faber, 1968.
    1833. Notebook 1967-68. New York: Farrar, Straus, 1969.
    1834. Notebook. New York: Farrar, Straus, and London: Faber, 1970.
    1835. The dolphin. New York: Farrar, Straus, 1973.
    1836. Lizzie and Harriet. New York: Farrar, Straus, 1973.
    1837. History. New York: Farrar, Straus, 1973.

LOWRY, Malcolm
    1838. Selected poems. San Francisco: City Lights, 1962.

LYONS, Richard
    1839. Men and tin kettles. Denver: Swallow, 1956.
    1840. One squeaking straw, eclogues. Fargo: North Dakota Institute for Regional Studies, 1958.
    1841. Public Journal, 1941-71. Fargo, ND: Scopcraft, 1972.

MacADAMS, Lewis
1842. City money. Oxford: Burning Water, 1966.
1843. Water charms. San Francisco: Dariel, 1968.
1844. The poetry room. New York: Harper & Row, 1970.
1845. Now let us eat of this pollen and place some on our
      heads, for we are to talk of it. New York: Harper
      & Row, 1973.

McAFEE, Thomas
1846. I'll be home late tonight. Columbia: University of
      Missouri Press, 1967.
1847. Rover youngblood. New York: Richard Baron, 1969.

McALEAVEY, Davis
1848. Sterling 403. Ithaca, NY: Ithaca House, 1971.

McALLISTER, Claire
1849. Arms of light, selected first poems. New York:
      Knopf, 1964.

McAULEY, James
1850. Draft balance sheet. New York: Oxford University
      Press, 1970.

McCARTHY, Eugene J.
1851. And time began. St. Paul, MN: North Central, 1968.
1852. Other things and the aardvark. Garden City, NY:
      Doubleday, 1970.

McCLOSKEY, Mark
1853. Goodbye, but listen. Nashville: Vanderbilt University
      Press, 1968.
1854. The sheen in flywings is what it comes to. Baltimore:
      Portfolio, 1972.

McCLURE, Michael
1855. Passage. Big Sur, CA: J. Williams, 1956.
1856. Peyote poem. San Francisco: Semina, 1958.
1857. For Artaud. New York: Totem, 1959.
1858. Hymns to St. Geryon, and other poems. San Francisco:
      Auerhahn, 1959; London: Cape Goliard, 1969.
1859. Dark brown. San Francisco: Auerhahn, 1961.
1860. The new book, a book of torture. New York: Grove,
      1961.
1861. Ghost tantras. San Francisco: City Lights, 1964.
1862. Thirteen mad sonnets. Milan: Serig Rafia Pezzoli,
      1964.
1863. Poisoned wheat. San Francisco: 1965.
1864. Love lion book. San Francisco: Four Seasons, 1966.
1865. Hail thee who play. Los Angeles: Black Sparrow,
      1968.
1866. The mammals. San Francisco: Cranium, 1968.
1867. The sermons of Jean Harlow and the curses of Billy the

Kid. San Francisco: Four Seasons, 1968.
1868. Little odes and the raptors. Los Angeles: Black Sparrow, 1969.
1869. Star. New York: Grove, 1970.
1870. Rare angel. Los Angeles: Black Sparrow, 1973.

McCORD, Howard
1871. The Spanish dark, and other poems. Seattle: University of Washington Press, 1965.
1872. Fables and transfigurations. San Francisco: Kayak, c. 1969.
1873. The five visions. San Francisco: Twowindows, 1970.
1874. Maps; poems toward an iconography of the West. Santa Cruz, CA: Kayak, 1971.
1875. Mirrors. Ithaca, NY: Stone Marrow, 1973.
1876. The diary of a lost girl. Northwood Narrows, NH: Lillabulero, 1972.

McCULLOUGH, Ken
1877. Migrations. Ithaca, NY: Stone Marrow, 1972.

McDONALD, Barry
1878. The pink house. Crete, NE: Best Cellar, 1972.

MacDONALD, Cynthia
1879. Amputations. New York: Braziller, 1972.

McDONALD, Maurice
1880. The homing elephant & cucumber prophesy party. San Francisco: Twowindows, 1967.
1881. The milk-shine curry easy buzzard reader. San Francisco: Twowindows, 1970.

McGAUGH, Lawrence
1882. A fifth Sunday. Berkeley: Oyez, 1965.
1883. Vacuum Cantos. Berkeley: Oyez, 1969.

McGRATH, Thomas
1884. First manifesto. Denver: Swallow and Critchlow, 1940.
1885. The dialectics of love. Prairie City, IL: Decker, 1944.
1886. To walk a crooked mile. Denver: Swallow, 1947.
1887. Longshot O'Leary's garland of practical poesie. New York: International, 1949.
1888. A witness to the times. Los Angeles: privately printed, 1953.
1889. Figures from a double world. Denver: Swallow, 1955.
1890. Letter to an imaginary friend. Denver: Swallow, 1962.
1891. New and selected poems. Denver: Swallow, 1964.
1892. Letter to an imaginary friend, parts I & II. Chicago: Swallow, 1970.
1893. The movie at the end of the world: collected poems. Chicago: Swallow, 1972.

McINTOSH, Sandy
    1894.   Earth works. Brooklyn, NY: Long Island University Press, 1970.

McKEOWN, Tom
    1895.   Alewife summer. Albuquerque: Road Runner, 1967.
    1896.   Drunk all afternoon. Madison, WI: Abraxas, 1969.
    1897.   Last thoughts. Madison, WI: Abraxas, 1969.
    1898.   The windsox of the calendar. Albuquerque: Road Runner, 1969.
    1899.   The milk of the wolf. Columbia, MO: Asari, 1970.
    1900.   The cloud keeper. Dublin: Seafront, 1972.
    1901.   The luminous revolver. Fremont, MI: Sumac, 1973.

McLAUGHLIN, Bill
    1902.   Conspiracies of love and death. Columbus: Ohio State University Press, 1970.

MACLEOD, Norman
    1903.   Horizons of death. New York: Parnassus, 1934.
    1904.   Thanksgiving before November. New York: Parnassus, 1936.
    1905.   Bitter roots. New York: Smith & Durrell, 1941.
    1906.   We thank you all the time. Prairie City, IL: Decker, 1941.
    1907.   A man in midpassage; collected poems, 1930-1947. Columbus, OH: Cronos, 1947.
    1908.   Pure as nowhere. Columbus, OH: Golden Goose, 1952.

MacLOW, Jackson
    1909.   August light poems. New York: Caterpillar, 1967.
    1910.   22 light poems. Los Angeles: Black Sparrow, 1968.
    1911.   23rd light poem/7th poem for Larry Eigner. London: Tetrad, 1969.
    1912.   The pronouns--a collection of 40 dances--for the dancers--6 February-22 March 1964. New York: Jackson MacLow, 1964; London: Tetrad, 1970.
    1913.   Stanzas for Iris Lezak. Barton, NY: Something Else, 1971.

McMAHON, Bryan
    1914.   Kree. Flushing, NY: New Voices, 1972.

McMICHAEL, James
    1915.   Against the falling evil. Chicago: Swallow, 1971.

McNEILL, Louise
    1916.   Mountain White. Dallas: Kaleidoscope, 1931.
    1917.   Gauley Mountain. New York: Harcourt, Brace, 1939.
    1918.   Time is our house. Bread Loaf, VT: Middlebury College Press, 1942.
    1919.   Hill-daughter. Charleston, WV: MHC Publications, 1971.

1920.   Paradox hill; from Appalachia to lunar shore.   Morgan-
        town: West Virginia University Library, 1972.

McPHERSON, Sandra
1921.   Elegies for the hot season.   Bloomington: Indiana Uni-
        versity Press, 1970.
1922.   Radiation.   New York: Ecco, 1973.

MADGETT, Naomi
1923.   One and the many.   New York: Exposition, 1956.
1924.   Star by star.   Detroit: Evenill, 1970.
1925.   Pink ladies in the afternoon.   Detroit: Lotus, 1972.

MAGOWAN, Robin
1926.   Voyages.   Santa Cruz, CA: Kayak, 1966.
1927.   Persian notes.   Berkeley: Futharc/Serendipity, 1972.

MAHONE, Barbara
1928.   Sugarfields.   Detroit: Broadside, 1970.

MAJOR, Clarence
1929.   Love poems of a Black man.   Omaha: Coercion, 1964.
1930.   Human juices.   Omaha: Coercion, 1965.
1931.   Swallow the lake.   Middletown, CT: Wesleyan Univer-
        sity Press, 1970.
1932.   Private line.   Detroit: Broadside, 1971.
1933.   Symptoms & madness.   New York: Corinth, 1971.
1934.   The syncopated cakewalk.   New York: Barlenmir
        House, 1972.

MALANGA, Gerard
1935.   Prelude to international velvet debutante.   Milwaukee:
        Great Lakes Books, 1967.
1936.   3 poems for Benedetta Barzini.   New York: Angel Hair:
        1967.
1937.   The last Benedetta poems.   Los Angeles: Black Spar-
        row, 1969.
1938.   10 poems for 10 poets.   Los Angeles: Black Sparrow,
        1970.
1939.   Poetry on film.   Norwood, PA: Telegraph Books, 1973.
1940.   Wheels of light.   Los Angeles: Black Sparrow, 1973.

MARCUS, Adrianne
1941.   The moon is a marrying eye.   Charlotte, NC: Red
        Clay, 1972.

MARCUS, Mordecai
1942.   Five minutes to noon.   Crete, NE: Best Cellar, 1971.

MARCUS, Morton
1943.   Origins.   Santa Cruz, CA: Kayak, 1967.
1944.   The Santa Cruz Mt. poems.   Santa Barbara: Capra,
        1972.

1945. Where the ocean covers us. Santa Barbara: Capra,
       1972.

MARKS, S. J.
1946. Lines. Iowa City: Cummington, 1973.

MARSHALL, Jack
1947. The darkest continent. New York: For Now, 1967.
1948. Bearings. New York: Harper & Row, 1969.
1949. Surviving in America. Iowa City: Cedar Creek Press,
       1972.

MATCHETT, William
1950. Water ouzel, and other poems. Boston: Houghton Mif-
       flin, 1955.
1951. Your house is on fire and your children are gone.
       Seattle: Consumption, 1970.

MATSON, Clive
1952. Mainline to the heart. Kerhonkson, NY: Poets Press,
       1966.
1953. Heroin. Berkeley: Neon Sun, 1972.

MATTHEWS, Jack
1954. An almanac for twilight. Chapel Hill: University of
       North Carolina Press, 1966.

MATTHEWS, William
1955. Broken syllables. Northwood Narrows, NH: Lilla-
       bulero, 1969.
1956. Ruining the new road. New York: Random House,
       1970.
1957. The cloud. Boston: Barn Dream, 1971.
1958. Sleek for the long flight; new poems. New York: Ran-
       dom House, 1972.
1959. An oar in the old water: poems in one line. Ithaca,
       NY: Stone, 1973.

MATTHIAS, John
1960. Bucyrus. Chicago: Swallow, 1971.

MATTINGLY, George
1961. The beginning of the wind. Iowa City: Blue Wind,
       1972.

MAY, James Boyer
1962. Selected poems, 1950-1955. San Francisco: Inferno,
       1955.
1963. Collected later poems. London: Villiers, 1957.

MAYER, Bernadette
1964. Moving. New York: Angel Hair, 1971.

MAYO, Edward L.
    1965. The diver. Minneapolis: University of Minnesota
           Press, 1947.
    1966. The center is everywhere. New York: Twayne, 1954.
    1967. Summer unbound, and other poems. Minneapolis: Uni-
           versity of Minnesota Press, 1958.

MAZZARO, Jerome
    1968. Changing the windows. Athens: Ohio University Press,
           1966.
    1969. Intrepid 17. Buffalo: Intrepid, 1970.

MELENDEZ, Jesus Papoleto
    1970. Street Poetry. New York: Barlenmir House, 1972.

MELHAM, D. H.
    1971. Notes on 94th street. New York: Poets Press, 1972.

MELNICK, David
    1972. Eclogs. Ithaca, NY: Ithaca House, 1972.

MELTZER, David
    1973. Ragas. San Francisco: Discovery Books, 1959.
    1974. The clown. Larkspur, CA: Semina, 1960.
    1975. We all have something to say to each other. San Fran-
           cisco: Auerhahn, 1962.
    1976. The process. Berkeley: Oyez, 1965.
    1977. The dark continent. Berkeley: Oyez, 1967.
    1978. Journal of the birth. Berkeley: Oyez, 1967.
    1979. Abulafia song. Santa Barbara: Unicorn, 1969.
    1980. From Eden book. Mill Valley, CA: Maya Quarto,
           1969.
    1981. Round the poem box; rustic & domestic home movies
           for Stan & Jane Brakhage. Los Angeles: Black
           Sparrow, 1969.
    1982. Yesod. London: Trigram, 1969.
    1983. Greenspeech. Santa Barbara: Christopher's Books,
           1970.
    1984. Letters & numbers. Berkeley: Oyez, 1970.
    1985. Luna. Los Angeles: Black Sparrow, 1970.
    1986. Hero/Lil. Los Angeles: Black Sparrow, 1971.
    1987. Birth. New York: Ballantine, 1972.
    1988. The eyes, the blood. San Francisco: Mudra, 1973.
    1989. French broom. Berkeley: Oyez, 1973.
    1990. Tens: selected poems 1961-1971. New York: McGraw-
           Hill, 1973.

MENASHE, Samuel
    1991. No Jerusalem but this. New York: October House,
           1971.

MENDELSON, Chaim
    1992. Views at a window: an alphabet. Belmont, MA:
           Hellric, 1971.

MEREDITH, William
    1993. Love letter from an impossible land. New Haven:
           Yale University Press, 1944.
    1994. Ships and other figures. Princeton: Princeton Univer-
           sity Press, 1948.
    1995. The open sea, and other poems. New York: Knopf,
           1958.
    1996. The wreck of the Thresher, and other poems. New
           York: Knopf, 1964.
    1997. Earth walk: new and selected poems. New York:
           Knopf, 1970.

MERRILL, James
    1998. The black swan. Athens: Icaros, 1946.
    1999. First poems. New York: Knopf, 1951.
    2000. Short stories. Pawlet, VT: Banyan, 1954.
    2001. The country of a thousand years of peace, and other
           poems. New York: Knopf, 1959.
    2002. Selected poems. London: Chatto and Windus, 1961.
    2003. Water Street. New York: Atheneum, 1962.
    2004. Nights and days. New York: Atheneum, and London:
           Chatto & Windus, 1966.
    2005. The thousand and second night. Athens: Editions $8\frac{1}{2}$,
           1966.
    2006. The fire screen. New York: Atheneum, 1969; London:
           Chatto and Windus, 1970.
    2007. The country of a thousand years of peace, and other
           poems. Rev. ed. New York: Atheneum, 1970.
    2008. Braving the elements. New York: Atheneum, 1972.
    2009. Two poems: from the Cupola, [and] the summer peo-
           ple. London: Chatto and Windus, 1972.

MERTON, Thomas
    2010. Selected poems. London: Hollis & Carter, 1950, enl.
           ed. New York: New Directions, 1967.
    2011. The strange islands. New York: New Directions, 1957.
    2012. Selected poems. New York: J. Laughlin, 1959.
    2013. The behavior of Titans. New York: New Directions,
           1961.
    2014. Emblems of a season of fury. Norfolk, CT: J.
           Laughlin, 1963.
    2015. Landscape, prophet and wild-dog. Syracuse, NY, 1968.
    2016. The geography of Lograire. New York: New Direc-
           tions, 1969.
    2017. Thomas Merton: early poems/1940-42. Lexington,
           KY: Anvil, 1971.

MERWIN, William S.
    2018. A mask for Janus. New Haven: Yale University Press,
           1952.
    2019. The dancing bears. New Haven: Yale University Press,
           1954.
    2020. Green with beasts. New York: Knopf, and London:
           Rupert-Hart-Davis, 1956.

2021. The drunk in the furnace.   New York: Macmillan,
        and London: Rupert-Hart-Davis, 1960.
2022. The moving target.   New York: Atheneum, 1963; Lon-
        don: Rupert-Hart-Davis, 1967.
2023. The lice.   New York: Atheneum, and London: Rupert-
        Hart-Davis, 1967.
2024. Three poems.   New York: Phoenix Book Shop, 1968.
2025. Animae.   San Francisco: Kayak, 1969.
2026. The carrier of ladders.   New York: Atheneum, 1970.
2027. A new right arm.   Albuquerque: Road Runner, 1970.
2028. Japanese figures.   Santa Barbara: Unicorn, 1971.
2029. The miner's pale children.   New York: Atheneum,
        1971.
2030. Asian figures.   New York: Atheneum, 1973.
2031. Writings to an unfinished accompaniment.   New York:
        Atheneum, 1973.

MESCHERY, Tom
2032. Over the rim.   New York: McCall, 1970.

METCALF, Paul C.
2033. Patagoni.   New York: Jargon, 1971.

MEYERS, Bert
2034. Early rain.   Denver: Swallow, 1960.
2035. The dark birds.   Garden City, NY: Doubleday, 1968.

MEYERS, Joan Simpson
2036. Poetry and a libretto.   Denver: Swallow, 1965.

MEZEY, Robert
2037. The wandering Jew; autobiographical poem.   Mount
        Vernon, IA: Hillside Press, 1960.
2038. The lovemaker.   Iowa City: Cummington, 1961.
2039. White blossoms.   West Branch, IA: Cummington, 1965.
2040. The mercy of sorrow.   Philadelphia: Three People,
        1966.
2041. A book of dying.   Santa Cruz, CA: Kayak, 1969.
2042. The door standing open; new and selected poems, 1954-
        1969.   Boston: Houghton Mifflin, and London: Ox-
        ford University Press, 1970.

MICHELSON, Peter
2043. The eater.   Chicago: Swallow, 1972.

MICOU, Regina see IFETAYO, Femi Funmi

MILES, Josephine
2044. Lines at intersections.   New York: Macmillan, 1939.
2045. Poems on several occasions.   Norfolk, CT: New
        Directions, 1941.
2046. Local measures.   New York: Reynal and Hitchock,
        1946.

83   Miller

2047. Prefabrications. Bloomington: Indiana University
      Press, 1955.
2048. Poems, 1930-1960. Bloomington: Indiana University
      Press, 1960.
2049. Civil poems. Berkeley: Oyez, 1966.
2050. Kinds of affection. Middletown, CT: Wesleyan Univer-
      sity Press, 1967.
2051. Fields of learning. Berkeley: Oyez, 1972.

MILLER, Brown
2052. Nine seasons in paradise and other tortures. Monterey,
      CA: Polygon, 1967.
2053. Fertilized brains. San Francisco: Open Skull, 1968.
2054. 33 phases of the fatal stroboscope. Sacramento:
      Runcible Spoon, 1968.
2055. Waters & shadows. San Francisco: Twowindows, 1969.
2056. The world is coming! Sacramento: Runcible Spoon,
      1969.

MILLER, Heather Ross
2057. Tenants of the house. New York: Harcourt, Brace,
      1966.
2058. The wind southerly. New York: Harcourt, Brace,
      1967.

MILLER, Jason
2059. Stone step. New York: Jadis/Yumi, 1968.
2060. That championship season. New York: Atheneum,
      1972.

MILLER, Vassar
2061. Adam's footprint. New Orleans: New Orleans Poetry
      Journal, 1956.
2062. Wage war on silence, a book of poems. Middletown,
      CT: Wesleyan University Press, 1960.
2063. My bones being wiser. Middletown, CT: Wesleyan
      University Press, 1963.
2064. Onions and roses. Middletown, CT: Wesleyan Univer-
      sity Press, 1968.

MILLS, Barriss
2065. Parvenus & ancestors. New York: Sparrow, 1959.
2066. Domestic fables. New Rochelle, NY: Elizabeth, 1971.

MILLS, Ralph
2067. Cry of the human. Chicago: Swallow, 1973.

MILLWARD, Pamela
2068. The route of the phoebe snow. San Francisco: Coyote
      Books, 1966.
2069. Once and for all. San Francisco: Four Seasons,
      1969.

MILTON, John R.
    2070. The loving hawk. Fargo: North Dakota Institute of Regional Studies, 1962.
    2071. The tree of bones. Mankato, MN: Verb, 1965.
    2072. This lonely house. Minneapolis: James Thueson, 1968.
    2073. The tree of bones and other poems. Vermillion: University of South Dakota Press, 1973.

MINTZ, Ruth Finer
    2074. The darkening green. Denver: Swallow, 1965.

MITCHELL, David
    2075. Wrecks and other poems. Binghamton, NY: Bellevue, 1973.

MITCHELL, Roger
    2076. Letters from Siberia & other poems. New York: New Rivers, 1972.

MOEBIUS, William
    2077. Elegies & odes. Chicago: Swallow, 1969.

MOFFITT, John
    2078. The living seed. New York: Harcourt, Brace, 1962.

MONTGOMERY, Marion
    2079. Dry lightning. Lincoln: University of Nebraska Press, 1960.
    2080. Stones from the rubble. Campobello, SC: Argus Books, 1965.
    2081. The gull, and other Georgia scenes. Athens: University of Georgia Press, 1970.

MOONEY, Stephen
    2082. News from the South. Knoxville: University of Tennessee Press, 1966.

MOORE, Daniel
    2083. Dawn visions. San Francisco: City Lights, 1963.
    2084. Burnt heart; ode to the war dead. San Francisco: City Lights, 1971.
    2085. By Selkirk's Lake & other poems. Ithaca, NY: Ithaca House, 1971.

MOORE, Richard
    2086. A question of survival. Athens: University of Georgia Press, 1971.
    2087. Word from the hills: a sonnet sequence in 4 movements. Athens: University of Georgia Press, 1972.

MOORE, Ruth
    2088. Cold as a dog and the wind northeast. New York: Morrow, 1958.

2089. Time's web. New York: Morrow, 1972.

MORGAN, Frederick
2090. A book of change. New York: Scribner, 1972.

MORGAN, Robert
2091. Zirconia poems. Northwood Narrows, NH: Lillabulero,
         1969.
2092. Red owl. New York: Norton, 1972.

MORGAN, Robin
2093. Monster. New York: Random House, 1973.

MORRIS, Charles
2094. Festival. New York: Braziller, 1966.

MORRIS, Harry
2095. The sorrowful city. Gainesville: University of Florida
         Press, 1965.
2096. Birth, and copulation, and death. Tallahassee:
         Florida State University Press, 1969.
2097. The snake hunter. Athens: University of Georgia
         Press, 1970.

MORRIS, John N.
2098. Green business. New York: Atheneum, 1970.

MORRISON, Jim
2099. The lords and the new creatures. New York: Simon
         and Schuster, 1970.

MORRISON, Lillian
2100. The ghosts of Jersey City, & other poems. New York:
         Crowell, 1967.
2101. Miranda's music. New York: Crowell, 1968.

MORRISON, Theodore
2102. The serpent in the cloud. Boston: Houghton Mifflin,
         1931.
2103. Notes of death and life. New York: Crowell, 1935.
2104. The devious way. New York: Viking, 1944.
2105. The dream of Alcestis. New York: Viking, 1950.
2106. To make a world. New York: Viking, 1957.

MORSE, Samuel French
2107. The scattered causes. Denver: Swallow, 1955.
2108. The changes. Denver: Swallow, 1964.

MOSES, W. R.
2109. Identities. Middletown, CT: Wesleyan University
         Press, 1965.

MOSS, Howard
    2110. The wound and the weather. New York: Reynal and
          Hitchcock, 1946.
    2111. The toy fair. New York: Scribner, 1954.
    2112. A swimmer in the air. New York: Scribner, 1957.
    2113. A winter come, a summer gone; poems 1946-1960.
          New York: Scribner, 1960.
    2114. Finding them lost, and other poems. New York:
          Scribner, 1965.
    2115. Second nature. New York: Atheneum, 1968.
    2116. Selected poems. New York: Atheneum, 1971.

MOSS, Stanley
    2117. The wrong angel. New York: Macmillan, 1966.
    2118. The wrong angel and new poems. London: Anvil
          Press, 1969.

MUELLER, Lisel
    2119. Dependencies. Chapel Hill: University of North Caro-
          lina Press, 1965.
    2120. Life of a queen. La Crosse, WI: Juniper, 1970.

MUHAJIR, El see X, Marvin

MURPHY, Richard
    2121. Battle of Aughrim. New York: Knopf, 1968.

MUSTAPHA, Mukhtarr
    2122. Thorns and thistles. Detroit: Broadside, 1972.

NAMEROFF, Rochelle
    2123. Body prints. Ithaca, NY: Ithaca House, 1972.

NANDY, Pritish
    2124. From the outer banks of the Brahmaputra. New York:
          New Rivers, 1969.

NASH, Ogden
    2125. Free wheeling. New York: Simon and Schuster, 1931.
    2126. Hard lines. New York: Simon and Schuster, 1931;
          London: Duckworth, 1932.
    2127. The primrose path. New York: Simon and Schuster,
          1935; London: J. M. Dent, 1937.
    2128. I'm a stranger here myself. Boston: Little, Brown,
          and London: Victor Gollancz, 1938.
    2129. The face is familiar. Boston: Little, Brown, 1940;
          London: Dent, 1943.
    2130. Good intentions. Boston: Little, Brown, 1942; London:
          Dent, 1943.
    2131. Many long years ago. Boston: Little, Brown, 1945;
          London: Dent, 1954.

2132. Selected verse. New York: Modern Library, 1946.
2133. Versus. Boston: Little, Brown, and London: Dent,
       1949.
2134. Family reunion. Boston: Little, Brown, 1950; London:
       Dent, 1951.
2135. The private dining room, and other new verses. Bos-
       ton: Little, Brown, and London: Dent, 1953.
2136. Parents keep out: elderly poems for younger readers.
       Boston: Little, Brown, 1951; London: Dent, 1962.
2137. The pocket book of Ogden Nash. New York: Pocket
       Books, 1954.
2138. The Christmas that almost wasn't. Boston: Little,
       Brown, 1957; London: Dent, 1958.
2139. You can't get there from here. Boston: Little, Brown,
       and London: Dent, 1957.
2140. Custard, the dragon. Boston: Little, Brown, 1959;
       London: Dent, 1960.
2141. Verses from 1929 on. Boston: Little, Brown, 1959;
       London: Dent, 1961.
2142. A boy is a boy; the fun of being a boy. New York:
       Franklin Watts, 1960; London: Dent, 1961.
2143. Scrooge rides again. Berkeley: Hart, 1960.
2144. [no entry]
2145. Everyone but thee and me. Boston: Little, Brown,
       1962; London: Dent, 1963.
2146. The new nutcracker suite and other innocent verses.
       Boston: Little, Brown, 1962.
2147. The adventures of Isabel. Boston: Little, Brown,
       1963.
2148. A boy and his room. New York: Franklin Watts, 1963.
2149. A boy and his room and the adventures of Isabel. Lon-
       don: Dent, 1964.
2150. Marriage lines; notes of a student husband. Boston:
       Little, Brown, and London: Dent, 1964.
2151. Girls are silly. New York: Franklin Watts, 1962;
       London: Dent, 1964.
2152. The untold adventures of Santa Claus. Boston: Little,
       Brown, 1964; London: Dent, 1965.
2153. An Ogden Nash omnibook. London: Dent, 1967.
2154. The mysterious ouphe. Eau Claire, WI: E. M. Hale,
       1967.
2155. [no entry]
2156. There's always another windmill. Boston: Little,
       Brown, 1968.
2157. Bed riddance; a posy for the indisposed. Boston:
       Little, Brown, 1969.
2158. The animal garden. London: Deutsch, 1972.
2159. The cruise of the aardvark. London: Deutsch, 1972.
2160. The old dog barks backwards. Boston: Little, Brown,
       1972.

NATHAN, Leonard
    2161. Glad and sorry seasons. New York: Random House,

1963.
2162. Western reaches. San Jose, CA: Talisman, 1958.
2163. The matchmaker's lament and other astonishments.
Northampton, MA: Gehenna, 1967.
2164. The day the perfect speakers left. Middletown, CT:
Wesleyan University Press, 1969.
2165. Flight plan. Berkeley: Cedar Hill, 1971.

NATHAN, Robert
2166. The married man. New York: Knopf, 1962.
2167. Evening song: selected poems 1950-1973. San Fran-
cisco: Capra, 1973.

NELSON, Paul
2168. Cargo. Iowa City: Stone Wall, 1972.

NELSON, Stanley
2169. The passion of Tammuz. Florence: Bellosquardo
Press, 1959.
2170. The Brooklyn book of the dead. New York: The Smith,
1971.

NEMEROV, Howard
2171. The image and the law. New York: Holt, 1947.
2172. Guide to the ruins. New York: Random House, 1950.
2173. The salt garden. Boston: Atlantic-Little, Brown, 1955.
2174. Mirrors and windows. Chicago: University of Chicago
Press, 1958.
2175. New & selected poems. Chicago: University of Chica-
go Press, 1960.
2176. The next room of the dream. Chicago: University of
Chicago Press, 1962.
2177. The blue swallows. Chicago: University of Chicago
Press, 1967.
2178. The winter lightning; selected poems. London: Rapp
and Whiting, 1968.
2179. Gnomes and occasions. Chicago: University of Chi-
cago Press, 1973.

NEWMAN, Louis
2180. Pebbles & sand. New York: The Smith, 1973.

NEWMAN, Paul Baker
2181. The cheetah and the fountain. Fort Smith, AR: South
and West, 1968.
2182. Dust of the sun. Fort Smith, AR: South and West,
1969.
2183. The ladder of love. New York: The Smith, 1970.

NEWTH, Rebecca
2184. Xeme. Fremont, MI: Sumac, 1971.

NICHOLES, Marion
   2185. Life styles. Detroit: Broadside, 1971.

NICHOLS, Robert
   2186. Slow newsreel of man riding train. San Francisco:
         City Lights, 1962.

NICKLAUS, Frederick
   2187. The man who bit the sun. New York: New Directions,
         1964.

NIMS, John Frederick
   2188. The iron pastoral. New York: Sloane, 1947.
   2189. A fountain in Kentucky, and other poems. New York:
         Sloane, 1950.
   2190. Knowledge of the evening; poems, 1950-1960. New
         Brunswick, NJ: Rutgers University Press, 1960.
   2191. Of flesh and bone. New Brunswick, NJ: Rutgers Uni-
         versity Press, 1967.

NOLL, Bink
   2192. The center of the circle. New York: Harcourt, Brace,
         1962.
   2193. The feast. New York: Harcourt, Brace, 1967.

NORMAN, Charles
   2194. The bright world. New York: Morrow, 1930.
   2195. The savage century. Prairie City, IL: Decker, 1942.
   2196. Soldier's diary. New York: Scribner, 1944.
   2197. Selected poems. New York: Macmillan, 1962.
   2198. The portents of the air. Indianapolis: Bobbs-Merrill,
         1973.
   2199. [no entry]

NORRIS, Kathleen
   2200. Falling off. Chicago: Big Table, 1971.

NORSE, Harold
   2201. The undersea mountain. Denver: Swallow, 1953.
   2202. The dancing beasts. New York: Macmillan, 1962.
   2203. Karma circuit. London: Nothing Doing in London
         Press, 1967.

OATES, Joyce Carol
   2204. Women in love, and other poems. New York: Albondo-
         cani, 1968.
   2205. Anonymous sins & other poems. Baton Rouge: Louisi-
         ana State University Press, 1969.
   2206. Love and its derangements. Baton Rouge: Louisiana
         State University Press, 1970.
   2207. Angel fire. Baton Rouge: Louisiana State University
         Press, 1973.

O'CONNELL, Richard
  2208. Deaths and distances. Philadelphia: Atlantis Editions,
         1965.
  2209. Brazilian happenings. Philadelphia: Atlantis Editions,
         1966.
  2210. Terrane. Baltimore: Contemporary Poetry, 1967.
  2211. Thirty epigrams. Philadelphia: Atlantis Editions,
         1971.

O'GORMAN, Ned
  2212. The night of the hammer. New York: Harcourt,
         Brace, 1959.
  2213. Adam before his mirror. New York: Harcourt, Brace,
         1961.
  2214. The buzzard and the peacock. New York: Harcourt,
         Brace, 1964.
  2215. The harvesters' vase. New York: Harcourt, Brace,
         1968.
  2216. The flag the hawk flies. New York: Knopf, 1972.

O'HARA, Frank
  2217. A city winter, and other poems. 1952.
  2218. Meditations in an emergency. Majorca: M. Alcover,
         1956; New York: Grove, 1957.
  2219. Odes. New York: Tiber, 1960.
  2220. Second Avenue. New York: Totem, 1960.
  2221. Lunch poems. San Francisco: City Lights, 1964.
  2222. Love poems (tentative title). 1965.
  2223. In memory of my feelings; a selection of poems. New
         York: Museum of Modern Art, 1967.
  2224. The collected poems of Frank O'Hara. New York:
         Knopf, 1971.

OLIVER, Mary
  2225. No voyage, and other poems. London: Dent, 1963;
         Boston: Houghton Mifflin, 1965.
  2226. The River Styx, Ohio, and other poems. New York:
         Harcourt, Brace, 1972.

OLSON, Charles
  2227. To Corrado Cagli. New York: Knoedler Gallery, 1947.
  2228. Y and X. Washington: Black Sun, 1950.
  2229. Letter for Melville. Black Mountain College, NC,
         1951.
  2230. This. Black Mountain College, NC, 1952.
  2231. In cold hell, in thicket. Majorca: Divers, and Dor-
         chester, MA: Origin, 1953.
  2232. The Maximus poems 1-10. Highlands, NC: Jargon,
         1953.
  2233. The Maximus poems 11-22. Highlands, NC: Jargon,
         1956.
  2234. O'Ryan. San Francisco: White Rabbit, 1958.
  2235. The distances. London: Grove, 1960; New York:

Grove, 1961.
2236.   The Maximus poems. New York: Jargon, and London:
        Centaur, 1960.
2237.   Maximus, from Dogtown I. San Francisco: Auerhahn,
        1961.
2238.   O'Ryan 1, 2, 3, 4, 5, 6, 7, 8, 9, 10. San Francisco:
        White Rabbit, 1965.
2239.   Proprioception. San Francisco: Four Seasons, 1965.
2240.   Maximus poems IV, V, VI. London: Cape Goliard,
        and New York: Grossman, 1968.
2241.   Archaeologist of morning. New York: Grossman, and
        London: Cape Goliard, 1970.

OLSON, Elder
2242.   Thing of sorrow. New York: Macmillan, 1934.
2243.   The cock of heaven. New York: Macmillan, 1940.
2244.   The scarecrow Christ, and other poems. New York:
        Noonday, 1954.
2245.   Poems and plays, 1948-1958. Chicago: University of
        Chicago Press, 1958.
2246.   Collected poems. Chicago: University of Chicago
        Press, 1963.

OLSON, Toby
2247.   The hawk-foot poems. Madison, WI: Abraxas, 1969.
2248.   Worms into nails. Mt. Horeb, WI: Perishable Press,
        1969.
2249.   Maps. Mt. Horeb, WI: Perishable Press, 1970.
2250.   Vectors. Milwaukee: Ziggurat/Membrane, 1972.

OPPEN, George
2251.   Discrete series. New York: Objectivist, 1934.
2252.   The materials. New York: New Directions, 1962.
2253.   This in which. New York: New Directions, 1965.
2254.   Of being numerous. New York: New Directions, 1968.
2255.   Alpine. Mt. Horeb, WI: Perishable Press, 1969.
2256.   Seascape: needle's eye. Fremont, MI: Sumac, 1972.
2257.   Collected poems. London: Fulcrum, 1973.

OPPENHEIMER, Joel
2258.   The dancer. Highlands, NC: Jargon, 1952.
2259.   The dutiful son. Highlands, NC: J. Williams, 1956.
2260.   The love bit, and other poems. New York: Totem,
        1962.
2261.   Before a battle, and other poems. New York: Har-
        court, Brace, 1967.
2262.   Sirventes on a sad occurrence. Mt. Horeb, WI:
        Perishable Press, 1967.
2263.   In time; poems, 1962-1968. Indianapolis: Bobbs-
        Merrill, 1969.

ORLOVITZ, Gil
2264.   Concerning man. Pawlet, VT: Banyan, 1947.

2265. Keep to your belly. New York: Brigante, 1952.
2266. The diary of Dr. Eric Zeno. San Francisco: Inferno, 1953.
2267. The diary of Alexander Patience. San Francisco: Inferno, 1958.
2268. The papers of Professor Bold. Eureka, CA: Hearse, 1958.
2269. Selected poems. San Francisco: Inferno, 1960.
2270. Art of the sonnet. Nashville: Hillsboro, 1961.
2271. Couldn't say, might be love. London: Barrie and Rockliff, 1969.
2272. More poems. Fredericton, NB, Canada: Fred Cogswell, 1972.

ORLOVSKY, Peter
2273. Lepers cry. New York: Phoenix Bookshop, 1972.

ORR, Gregory
2274. Burning the empty nests. New York: Harper & Row, 1973

OSTRIKER, Alicia
2275. Songs. New York: Holt, Rinehart and Winston, 1969.
2276. Once more out of darkness. New York: The Smith, 1970.

OSTROFF, Anthony
2277. Imperatives. New York: Harcourt, Brace, 1962.

OWEN, Guy
2278. The white stallion, and other poems. Winston-Salem, NC: J. F. Blair, 1969.

OWENS, Rochelle
2279. Not be essence that cannot be. New York: Trobar, 1961.
2280. Salt and core. Los Angeles: Black Sparrow, 1968.
2281. I am the babe of Joseph Stalin's daughter; poems, 1961-1971. New York: Kulchur, 1972.
2282. Poems from Joe's garage. Providence, RI: Burning Deck, 1973.

PACK, Robert
2283. The irony of joy. New York: Scribner, 1955.
2284. A stranger's privilege. New York: Macmillan and Hessle, Yorkshire: Asphodel Books, 1959.
2285. Guarded by women. New York: Random House, 1963.
2286. Selected poems. London: Chatto and Windus, 1965.
2287. Nothing but light. New Brunswick, NJ: Rutgers University Press, 1972.

PADGETT, Ron (see also VEITCH, Tom)
   2288. In advance of the broken arm. New York: "C" Press,
       1964.
   2289. Sky. London: Goliard, 1966.
   2290. Tone arm. Brightlingsea, Essex: Once, 1967.
   2291. Great balls of fire. Chicago: Holt, Rinehart and
       Winston, 1969.

PALMER, Doug
   2292. Poems to the people. Berkeley: Peace and Gladness
       Co-op, 1965.
   2293. The quick and the quiet. Berkeley: Synapse, 1965.
   2294. Basta. Berkeley: Worthy Labor, 1967.
   2295. Margaret's experiences. Berkeley, OR, 1967.
   2296. Moon services. Berkeley: Worthy Labor, 1967.
   2297. In quire. Berkeley: Oyez, 1973.

PALMER, Michael
   2298. Plan of the city of O. Boston: Barn Dream, 1971.
   2299. Blake's Newton. Los Angeles: Black Sparrow, 1972.

PARKER, Stephen
   2300. A lifetime of happiness. Santa Cruz, CA: Kayak, 1971.

PARKINSON, Thomas
   2301. Men, women, vines. Berkeley: Ark, 1959.
   2302. Thanatos; earth poems. Berkeley: Oyez, 1965.

PARLATORE, Anselm
   2303. Provisions. Ithaca, NY: Stone Marrow, 1971.

PASTAN, Linda
   2304. A perfect circle of sun. Chicago: Swallow, 1971.

PATCHEN, Kenneth
   2305. Before the brave. New York: Random House, 1936.
   2306. First will and testament. New York: New Directions,
       1939.
   2307. The dark kingdom. New York: Harriss and Givens,
       1942.
   2308. Teeth of the lion. New York: New Directions, 1942.
   2309. Cloth of the tempest. New York: Harper, 1943.
   2310. An astonished eye looks out of the air. Waldport, OR:
       Untide, 1945.
   2311. Outlaw of the lowest planet. London: Grey Walls,
       1946.
   2312. Pictures of life and death. New York: Padell, 1947.
   2313. Selected poems. New York: New Directions, 1946;
       rev. 1958, 1964.
   2314. Panels for the walls of heaven. San Francisco: Bern
       Porter, 1947.
   2315. Red wine and yellow hair. New York: New Directions,
       1949.

2316. To say if you love someone.   Prairie City, IL: Deck-
       er, 1949.
2317. Orchards, thrones & caravans.   San Francisco: The
       Print Workshop, 1952.
2318. Fables and other little tales.   Karlsruhe: J. Williams,
       1953.
2319. The famous boating party, and other poems in prose.
       New York: New Directions, 1954.
2320. Poems of humor & protest.   San Francisco: City
       Lights, 1954.
2321. Glory never guesses.   Privately printed, 1955.
2322. Surprise for the bagpipe player.   Privately printed,
       1956.
2323. Hurrah for anything; poems & drawings.   Highlands,
       NC: J. Williams, 1957.
2324. When we were here together.   New York: New Direc-
       tions, 1957.
2325. Poemscapes.   Highlands, NC: J Williams, 1958.
2326. Because it is.   Norfolk, CT: J. Laughlin, 1960.
2327. Love poems.   San Francisco: City Lights, 1960.
2328. The journal of albion moonlight.   New York: New
       Directions, 1961.
2329. The moment.   Palo Alto, CA: privately printed, 1962.
2330. Doubleheader.   New York: New Directions, 1966.
2331. Hallelujah anyway.   New York: New Directions, 1966.
2332. But even so.   New York: New Directions, 1968.
2333. The collected poems of Kenneth Patchen.   New York:
       New Directions, 1968.
2334. Love and war poems.   Micleover, Derby: Whisper
       and Shout, 1968.
2335. Selected poems.   London: Cape, 1968.
2336. Aflame and afun of walking faces.   New York: New
       Directions, 1970.
2337. In quest of candlelighters.   New York: New Directions,
       1972.

PATTON, Rob
2338. Thirty-seven poems: one night stanzas.   Ithaca, NY:
       Ithaca House, 1971.

PAUKER, John
2339. Yoked by violence.   Denver: Swallow, 1949.
2340. Excellency.   Iowa City: Stone Wall, 1968.

PEARCE, Ellen
2341. Life in (very) minor works.   New York: October
       House, 1968.

PECK, Richard
2342. Pictures that storm inside my head.   New York: Holt,
       Rinehart and Winston, 1973.

PENDLETON, Conrad (Walter E. Kidd)
    2343. Slow fire of time. Denver: Swallow, 1956.
    2344. West: Manhattan to Oregon. Denver: Swallow, 1966.

PERCHIK, Simon
    2345. I counted only April. New Rochelle, NY: Elizabeth, 1964.
    2346. Twenty years of hands. New Rochelle, NY: Elizabeth, 1966.
    2347. Which hand holds the brother; poems, 1966-1968. New Rochelle, NY: Elizabeth, 1969.
    2348. Hands you are secretly wearing. New Rochelle, NY: Elizabeth, 1972.

PERKOFF, Stuart Z.
    2349. The suicide room. Karlsruhe: J. Williams, 1956.

PERLBERG, Mark
    2350. The burning field. New York: Morrow, 1970.

PERLMAN, John
    2351. Kachina. Columbus: Ohio State University Press, 1971.
    2352. Three years rings. New Rochelle, NY: Elizabeth, 1972.

PERREAULT, John
    2353. Camouflage. Cambridge, MA: Lines, 1966.
    2354. Luck. New York: Kulchur, 1969.

PERRY, Ronald
    2355. The fire nursery. Miami: Stamperia di Antonio, 1956.
    2356. The pipe smokers. Miami: Pandanus, 1959.
    2357. The rock harbor. Denver: Swallow, 1959.
    2358. Voyages from Troy. Miami: Mariner, 1962.

PETERFREUND, Stuart
    2359. The hanged knife, and other poems. Ithaca, NY: Ithaca House, 1970.

PETERS, Robert
    2360. The cry of the wanderer. New York: William-Frederick, 1952.
    2361. Song of death. New York: William-Frederick, 1952.
    2362. Songs for a son. New York: Norton, 1967.
    2363. The sow's head & other poems. Detroit: Wayne State University Press, 1968.
    2364. Connections: in the Lake District. London: Anvil Press, 1970.
    2365. Cool zebras of light. Santa Barbara: Christopher's, 1973.

PETERSEN, Donald
  2366. The spectral boy. Middletown, CT: Wesleyan University Press, 1964.

PETERSON, Robert
  2367. Home for the night. San Francisco: Bindweed, 1962.
  2368. The binnacle. Chapel Hill, NC: Lillabulero, 1967.
  2369. Wondering where you are. San Francisco: Kayak, 1969.

PETRIE, Paul
  2370. The facts of mercy. Ann Arbor, MI: University Microfilms, 1957.
  2371. Confessions of a non-conformist. Mount Vernon, IA: Hillside, 1963.
  2372. The race with time and the devil. Francestown, NH: Golden Quill, 1965.
  2373. From under the hill of night. Nashville: Vanderbilt University Press, 1969.

PFISTER, Arthur
  2374. Beer cans, bullets, things & pieces. Detroit: Broadside, 1972.

PHILBRICK, Charles H.
  2375. Wonderstrand revisited, a Cape Cod sequence. Sanbornville, NH: Wake-Book House, 1960.
  2376. New England suite; selected poems, 1950-1962. New York: Clarke and Way, 1962.
  2377. Voyages down, and other poems. New York: Harcourt, Brace, 1967.

PHILBRICK, Stephen
  2378. Seeds. Providence, RI: Hellcoal, 1970.

PIERCY, Marge
  2379. Breaking camp. Middletown, CT: Wesleyan University Press, 1968.
  2380. Hard loving. Middletown, CT: Wesleyan University Press, 1969.
  2381. To be of use. Garden City, NY: Doubleday, 1973.

PILLIN, William
  2382. Poems. Prairie City, IL: Decker, 1939.
  2383. Theory of silence. Los Angeles: George Yamada, 1949.
  2384. Dance without shoes. Francestown, NH: Golden Quill, 1956.
  2385. Passage after midnight. San Francisco: Inferno, 1958.
  2386. Pavanne for a fading memory. Denver: Swallow, 1963.
  2387. Everything falling. Santa Cruz, CA: Kayak, 1971.

PITCHFORD, Kenneth
  2388. The blizzard ape. New York: Scribner, 1958.
  2389. A suite of angels, and other poems. Chapel Hill: University of North Carolina Press, 1967.
  2390. Color photos of the atrocities. Boston: Atlantic Monthly, 1973.

PLANZ, Allen
  2391. Poor white and other poems. Lanham, MD: Goosetree, 1965.
  2392. Studsong. New York: Lower East, 1968.
  2393. A night for rioting. Chicago: Swallow, 1969.
  2394. Wild-craft. Chicago: Swallow, 1973.

PLATH, Sylvia
  2395. The colossus & other poems. London: Heinemann, 1960; New York: Knopf, 1962.
  2396. Ariel. London: Faber, 1965; New York: Harper & Row, 1966.
  2397. Uncollected poems. London: Turret Books, 1965.
  2398. Crossing the water; transitional poems. New York: Harper & Row, and London: Faber, 1971.
  2399. Crystal gazer and other poems. London: Rainbow, 1971.
  2400. Lyonnesse. London: Rainbow, 1971.
  2401. Winter trees. London: Faber, 1971; New York: Harper & Row, 1972.

PLUMLY, Stanley
  2402. In the outer dark. Baton Rouge: Louisiana State University Press, 1970.
  2403. How the plains Indians got horses. Crete, NE: Best Cellar, 1973.

PLUMPP, Sterling
  2404. Portable soul. Chicago: Third World, 1969.
  2405. Half Black, half Blacker. Chicago: Third World, 1970.
  2406. Black rituals. Chicago: Third World, 1972.

PLUTZIK, Hyam
  2407. Apples from Shinar; a book of poems. Middletown, CT: Wesleyan University Press, 1959.

PLYMELL, Charles
  2408. Apocalypse rose. San Francisco: Dave Haselwood, 1966.
  2409. Cherokee. Paris: Christian Bourgois, 1970.
  2410. Neon poems. Syracuse, NY: Atom Mind, 1970.
  2411. Last of the moccasins. San Francisco: City Lights, 1971.
  2412. Over the stage of Kansas. New York: Telephone Books, 1973.

POLITE, Carlene Hatcher
2413. The flagellants. New York: Farrar, Straus, 1967.

POLK, Brigid
2414. Scars. Norwood, PA: Telegraph, 1973.

POLLAK, Felix
2415. The castle and the flaw. New Rochelle, NY: Elizabeth, 1963.
2416. Say when. La Crosse, WI: Juniper, 1970.
2417. Ginkgo. New Rochelle, NY: Elizabeth, 1973.

POMEROY, Ralph
2418. Stills and movies. San Francisco: Gesture Books, 1961.
2419. The canaries as they are. Washington: Charioteer, 1965.
2420. In the financial district. New York: Macmillan, 1968.

POMMY-VEGA, Janine
2421. Poems to Fernando. San Francisco: City Lights, 1968.

POSNER, David
2422. The deserted altar, and other poems. New York: Harcourt, Brace, 1957.
2423. A rake's progress: a poem in five sections. London and New York: Lion & Unicorn, 1962.
2424. The dialogues. Los Angeles: Black Sparrow, 1969.

POULIN, A. L., Jr.
2425. In advent. New York: Dutton, 1972.

PRICE, Reynolds
2426. Late warning; four poems. New York: Albondocani, 1968.
2427. Torso of an archaic Apollo. New York: Albondocani, 1969.

PRITCHARD, N. H.
2428. The matrix; poems, 1960-1970. Garden City, NY: Doubleday, 1970.
2429. Eecchhooeess. New York: New York University Press, 1971.

PURDY, Al
2430. Hiroshima poems. Trumansburg, NY: Crossing Press, 1972.

QUASHA, George
2431. Somapoetics. Fremont, MI: Sumac, 1973.

QUENNEVILLE, Freda
    2432. The weave. Madison, WI: Abraxas, 1969.

QUIRK, Cathleen
    2433. The only child. Boston: Barn Dream, 1970.

RAAB, Lawrence
    2434. Mysteries of the horizon. Garden City, NY: Double-
        day, 1972.

RAFFEL, Burton
    2435. Mia poems. New York: October House, 1968.

RAGO, Henry
    2436. The travelers. Columbus, OH: Golden Goose, 1949.
    2437. A sky of late summer. New York: Macmillan, 1963.

RAKOSI, Carl
    2438. Selected poems. New York: New Directions, 1941.
    2439. Two poems. New York: Modern Editions, 1942.
    2440. Amulet. New York: New Directions, 1967.
    2441. Ere-voice. New York: New Directions, 1971.

RAMSEY, Jarold
    2442. Love in an earthquake. Seattle: University of Wash-
        ington Press, 1973.

RAMSEY, Paul
    2443. In an ordinary place. Raleigh, NC: Southern Poetry
        Review, 1965.
    2444. The doors; poems of 1968. Martin, TN: Tennessee
        Poetry Press, 1968.
    2445. A window for New York. San Francisco: Twowindows,
        1968.

RANDALL, Belle
    2446. 101 different ways of playing solitaire. Pittsburgh:
        University of Pittsburgh Press, 1973.

RANDALL, Dudley
    2447. Cities burning. Detroit: Broadside, 1968.
    2448. Love you. Detroit: Broadside, 1970.
    2449. More to remember; poems of four decades. Chicago:
        Third World, 1971.
    2450. After the killing. Detroit: Broadside, 1973.

RANDALL, James
    2451. Don't ask me who I am. Detroit: Broadside, 1970.
    2452. Cities and other disasters. Detroit: Broadside, 1973.

RANDALL, Julia
2453. The solstice tree. Baltimore: Contemporary Poetry, 1952.
2454. Mimic August. Baltimore: Contemporary Poetry, 1960.
2455. The Puritan carpenter. Chapel Hill: University of North Carolina Press, 1965.
2456. Adam's dream. New York: Knopf, 1969.

RANDALL, Margaret
2457. Ecstasy is a number. New York: Gutman Foundation, 1961.
2458. Poems of the glass. Cleveland: Renegade, 1964.
2459. Small sounds of the bass fiddle. Albuquerque: Duende, 1964.
2460. October. Mexico City: El Corno Emplumado, 1965.
2461. 25 stages of my spine. New Rochelle, NY: Elizabeth, 1967.
2462. Water I slip into at night. Mexico City: privately printed, 1967.
2463. Getting rid of blue plastic; selected poems. Calcutta: Dialogue, 1968.
2464. So many rooms has a house, but one roof. Nyack, NY: New Rivers, 1968.
2465. Part of the solution: portrait of a revolutionary. New York: New Directions, 1973.

RATNER, Rochelle
2466. A birthday of waters. New York: New Rivers, 1971.
2467. False trees. New York: New Rivers, 1973.

RATTI, John
2468. A remembered darkness. New York: Viking, 1969.

RAVEN, John
2469. Blues for Momma and other low down stuff. Detroit: Broadside, 1971.

RAY, David
2470. X-rays, a book of poems. Ithaca, NY: Cornell University Press, 1965.
2471. A hill in Oklahoma and other poems. Bookmark Press, n.d.
2472. Dragging the main; and other poems. Ithaca, NY: Cornell University Press, 1968.

REECE, Byron
2473. Bow down in Jericho. New York: Dutton, 1950.
2474. A song of joy, and other poems. New York: Dutton, 1952.
2475. The season of flesh. New York: Dutton, 1955.

REED, Ishmael
  2476. Catechism of D Neoamerican Hoodoo church. Detroit:
        Broadside, 1971.
  2477. Conjure: selected poems, 1963-1970. Amherst: Uni-
        versity of Massachusetts Press, 1972.
  2478. Chattanooga. New York: Random House, 1973.

REED, J. D.
  2479. Expressways. New York: Simon and Schuster, 1969.
  2480. Fatback odes. Fremont, MI: Sumac, 1972.

REES, Ennis
  2481. Poems. Columbia: University of South Carolina Press,
        1964.

REEVE, F. D.
  2482. In the silent stones. New York: Morrow, 1968.
  2483. The blue cat. New York: Farrar, Straus, 1972.

RENDLEMAN, Danny L.
  2484. Signals to the blind. Ithaca, NY: Ithaca House, 1972.

REXROTH, Kenneth
  2485. In what hour. New York: Macmillan, 1940.
  2486. The phoenix and the tortoise. New York: New Direc-
        tions, 1944.
  2487. The art of worldly wisdom. Prairie City, IL: Decker,
        1949.
  2488. The signature of all things; poems, songs, elegies,
        translations, and epigrams. New York: New Direc-
        tions, 1949.
  2489. The dragon and the unicorn. Norfolk, CT: New Direc-
        tions, 1952.
  2490. In defense of the earth. New York: New Directions,
        1956.
  2491. The homestead called Damascus. New York: New
        Directions, 1963.
  2492. Natural numbers; new and selected poems. Norfolk,
        CT: New Directions, 1963.
  2493. The collected shorter poems. New York: New Direc-
        tions, 1967.
  2494. The heart's garden, the garden's heart. Cambridge,
        MA: Pym-Randall, 1967.
  2495. The collected longer poems. New York: New Direc-
        tions, 1968.
  2496. The spark in the tinder on knowing. Cambridge, MA:
        Pym-Randall, 1968.
  2497. Poems. Santa Barbara: Unicorn, 1970.
  2498. Sky sea birds trees earth house beasts flowers. Los
        Angeles: Black Sparrow, 1973.

REXROTH, Mary
  2499. The coffee should be warm now. San Francisco: Two-
        windows, 1970.

REYES, Carlos
    2500. Ikabana. Sacramento: Grande Ronde, 1966.
    2501. Odes for every occasion. Sacramento: Runcible Spoon,
            1970.
    2502. "basking in the twenty five foot dream. " Santa Barbara:
            White Rabbit/Open Space, 1972.

REYNOLDS, Tim
    2503. Halflife; poems 1962-4. Cambridge, MA: Pym-
            Randall, 1964.
    2504. Ryoanji. New York: Harcourt, Brace, 1964.
    2505. Catfish goodbye. n. p. , Anubis, 1967.
    2506. Slocum. Santa Barbara: Unicorn, 1967.
    2507. Tlateloco: a sequence from Que. New York: Phoenix
            Book Shop, 1970.
    2508. Que. Cambridge, MA: H. Ferguson, 1971.

REZMERSKI, John Calvin
    2509. Held for questioning. Columbia: University of Missouri
            Press, 1969.

RICH, Adrienne
    2510. A change of world. New Haven: Yale University
            Press, 1951.
    2511. The diamond cutters, and other poems. New York:
            Harper, 1955.
    2512. Snapshots of a daughter-in-law; poems, 1954-1962.
            New York: Harper & Row, 1963; New York: Norton,
            1967; London: Chatto and Windus, 1970.
    2513. Necessities of life; poems, 1962-1965. New York:
            Norton, 1966.
    2514. Selected poems. London: Chatto and Windus, 1967.
    2515. Leaflets; poems, 1965-1968. New York: Norton, 1969.
    2516. The will to change; poems 1968-1970. New York:
            Norton, 1971.
    2517. Diving into the wreck. New York: Norton, 1973.

RIDING, Laura
    2518. The close chaplet. New York: Adelphi, and London:
            Hogarth, 1926.
    2519. Voltaire. London: Hogarth, 1927.
    2520. Love as love, death as death. London: Seizin, 1928.
    2521. Poems: a joking word. London: Cape, 1930.
    2522. Though gently. Majorca: Seizin, 1930.
    2523. Twenty poems less. Paris: Hours, 1930.
    2524. Laura and Francisca. Majorca: Seizin, 1931.
    2525. Poet: a lying word. London: Arthur Barker, 1933.
    2526. Americans. Los Angeles: Primavera, 1934.
    2527. The life of the dead. London: Arthur Barker, 1934.
    2528. Collected poems. New York: Random House, and
            London: Cassell, 1938.
    2529. Selected poems. London: Faber, 1970.
    2530. Selected poems; in five sets. New York: Norton, 1973.

RILEY, Peter
    2531. Strange family. Providence, RI: Burning Deck, 1973.

ROBBINS, Martin
    2532. A refrain of roses. Denver: Swallow, 1965.
    2533. A reply to the headlines (poems, 1965-1970). Chicago:
        Swallow, 1970.

ROBERSON, Ed
    2534. When thy king is a boy. Pittsburgh: University of
        Pittsburgh Press, 1970.

ROBERTS, Burgert
    2535. Spacewalks; poems for the moon age. New York:
        Harper & Row, 1971.

ROBERTS, Nancy see SARGENT, Elizabeth

ROBINS, Natalie S.
    2536. Wild lace. Denver: Swallow, 1960.
    2537. My father spoke of his riches. Denver: Swallow,
        1966.
    2538. The peas belong on the eye level. Chicago: Swallow,
        1971.

RODGERS, Carolyn
    2539. Paper soul. Chicago: Third World, 1968.
    2540. Songs of a blackbird. Chicago: Third World, 1969.

RODITI, Edouard Herbert
    2541. Poems 1928-1948. New York: New Directions, 1949.
    2542. New hieroglyphic tales. San Francisco: Kayak, 1968.

RODMAN, Selden
    2543. Mortal triumph. New York: Farrar, Straus, 1932.
    2544. Death of the hero. New York: Shorewood, 1964.

ROECKER, W. A.
    2545. Willamette. Phoenix: Baleen, 1970.
    2546. You know me. Fremont, MI: Sumac, 1973.

ROETHKE, Theodore
    2547. Open house and other poems. New York: Knopf, 1941.
    2548. The lost son & other poems. Garden City, NY:
        Doubleday, 1948; London: J. Lehmann, 1949.
    2549. Praise to the end! Garden City, NY: Doubleday, 1951.
    2550. The waking; poems, 1933-1953. Garden City, NY:
        Doubleday, 1953.
    2551. Words for the wind; the collected verse of Theodore
        Roethke. London: Secker & Warburg, 1957; Garden
        City, NY: Doubleday, 1958.
    2552. I am! says the lamb. Garden City, NY: Doubleday,
        1961.

2553.   Party at the zoo. New York: Collier, and London:
          Macmillan, 1963.
2554.   Sequence, sometimes metaphysical. Iowa City: Stone
          Wall, 1963.
2555.   The far field. Garden City, NY: Doubleday, 1964.
2556.   Collected poems. Garden City, NY: Doubleday, 1966.
2557.   Selected poems. London: Faber, 1969.

ROKEAH, David
2558.   Eyes in the rock. Chicago: Swallow, 1968.

ROOT, William Pitt
2559.   The storm and other poems. New York: Atheneum,
          1969.
2560.   Striking the dark air for music. New York: Atheneum,
          1973.

ROSELIEP, Raymond
2561.   The linen bands. Westminster, MD: Newman, 1961.
2562.   The small rain. Westminster, MD: Newman, 1963.
2563.   Love makes the air light. New York: Norton, 1965.

ROSEN, Kenneth
2564.   Whole horse. New York: Braziller, 1973.

ROSEN, Norma
2565.   Touching evil. New York: Harcourt, Brace, 1969.

ROSENBERG, James L.
2566.   A primer of kinetics. Denver: Swallow, 1961.

ROSENTHAL, David
2567.   Eyes on the street. New York: Barlenmir House,
          1973.

ROSENTHAL, M. L.
2568.   Blue boy on skates. New York and London: Oxford
          University Press, 1964.
2569.   Beyond power; new poems. New York and London:
          Oxford University Press, 1969.
2570.   The view from the peacock's tail. New York: Oxford
          University Press, 1972.

ROSS, David
2571.   Three ages of lake light. New York: Macmillan, 1962.

ROTHENBERG, Jerome
2572.   White sun black sun. New York: Hawk's Well, 1960.
2573.   The seven hells of the Higoku Zoshi. New York:
          Trobar, 1962.
2574.   Sightings I-IX. New York: Hawk's Well, 1964.
2575.   The Gorky poems. Mexico City: El Corno Emplumado,
          1966.

2576. Between 1960-1963. London: Fulcrum, 1967.
2577. Conversations. Los Angeles: Black Sparrow, 1968.
2578. Poems, 1964-1967. Los Angeles: Black Sparrow, 1968.
2579. Sightings I-IX; &, Red easy a color: poems. London: Circle, 1968.
2580. Poland 1931. Santa Barbara: Unicorn, 1969.
2581. Poems for the game of silence, 1960-1970. New York: Dial, 1971.
2582. Esther K. comes to America: 1931. Santa Barbara: Unicorn, 1973.

RUBIN, Larry
2583. The world's old way. Lincoln: University of Nebraska Press, 1962.
2584. Lanced in light poems. New York: Harcourt, Brace, 1967.

RUDNIK, Raphael
2585. A lesson from the cyclops, and other poems. New York: Random House, 1969.
2586. In the heart of our city. New York: Random House, 1973.

RUKEYSER, Muriel
2587. Theory of flight. New Haven: Yale University Press, 1935.
2588. U. S. 1. New York: Covici, 1938.
2589. A turning wind. New York: Viking, 1939.
2590. Wake island. Garden City, NY: Doubleday, 1942.
2591. Beast in view. Garden City, NY: Doubleday, 1944.
2592. The green wave. Garden City, NY: Doubleday, 1947.
2593. Elegies. Norfolk, CT: New Directions, 1949.
2594. Orpheus. San Francisco: Centaur, 1949.
2595. Selected poems. New York: New Directions, 1951.
2596. Body of waking. New York: Harper, 1958.
2597. Waterlily fire, poems, 1935-1962. New York: Macmillan, 1962.
2598. The outer banks. Santa Barbara: Unicorn, 1967.
2599. The speed of darkness. New York: Random House, 1968.
2600. 29 poems. London: Rapp and Whiting, 1970.
2601. 20 poems. London: Rapp and Whiting, 1972.
2602. Breaking open. New York: Random House, 1973.
2603. Own face diary. New York: Random House, 1973.

RUSSELL, Norman H.
2604. At the zoo. Smithtown, NY: JRD Publications, 1969.
2605. Night dog & other poems. Lawrence, KA: Cottonwood Review, 1971.
2606. Indian thoughts: the small songs of God. La Crosse, WI: Juniper Books, 1972.

RUTSALA, Vern
    2607. The window. Middletown, CT: Wesleyan University
           Press, 1964.
    2608. Small songs. Iowa City: Stone Wall, 1969.
    2609. The harmful state. Crete, NE: Best Cellar, 1971.

RYAN, John Allen
    2610. Rut. Santa Barbara: White Rabbit/Open Space, 1970.
    2611. Union onion. Santa Barbara: White Rabbit/Open Space,
           1970.

SAGOFF, Maurice
    2612. Shrinklits. Garden City, NY: Doubleday, 1971.

SALISBURY, Ralph J.
    2613. Ghost grapefruit, and other poems. Ithaca, NY:
           Ithaca House, 1972.

SALTMAN, Benjamin
    2614. Blue with blue. Chapel Hill, NC: Lillabulero, 1968.

SAMPERI, Frank
    2615. The prefiguration. New York: Grossman, 1971.
    2616. The fourth. New Rochelle, NY: Elizabeth, 1973.
    2617. Quadrifarian. New York: Grossman, 1973.

SANCHEZ, Sonia
    2618. Home coming. Detroit: Broadside, 1969.
    2619. We a baddDDD people. Detroit: Broadside, 1970.
    2620. It's a new day; poems for young brothas and sistuhs.
           Detroit: Broadside, 1971.

SANDBURG, Helga
    2621. The unicorns. New York: Dial, 1965.
    2622. To a new husband. New York: World, 1970.

SANDEEN, Ernest
    2623. Antennas of silence; first poems. Baltimore: Contem-
           porary Poetry, 1953.
    2624. Children and older strangers. South Bend: University
           of Notre Dame Press, 1962.

SANDERS, Ed
    2625. Poem from jail. San Francisco: City Lights, 1963.
    2626. The toe-queen poems. New York: Fuck You Press,
           1964.
    2627. Banana: an anthology of banana-erotic poems. New
           York: Fuck You Press, 1965.
    2628. The complete sex poems of Ed Sanders. New York:
           Fug-Press, 1965.
    2629. Peace eye. Buffalo, NY: Frontier, 1965.

2630.   King Lord--Queen freak.   Cleveland: Renegade, 1966.

SANDY, Stephen
  2631.   Caroms.   New York: Groton, 1960.
  2632.   Mary Baldwin.   Dublin: Dolmen, 1962.
  2633.   Stresses in the peaceable kingdom.   Boston: Houghton
             Mifflin, 1967.
  2634.   Japanese room.   Providence, RI: Hellcoal, 1969.
  2635.   Roofs.   Boston: Houghton Mifflin, 1971.

SAPPÉ, Arthur
  2636.   Of dust and sparrows.   New York: New York Univer-
             sity Press, 1970.

SARGENT, Elizabeth (Nancy Roberts)
  2637.   The African boy.   New York: Macmillan, 1963.
  2638.   Love poems of Elizabeth Sargent.   New York: New
             American Library, 1966.

SAROYAN, Aram
  2639.   Aram Saroyan.   New York: Random House, 1968.
  2640.   (Untitled).   New York: Kulchur, 1968.
  2641.   Pages.   New York: Random House, 1969.
  2642.   Words and photographs.   Chicago: Follett, 1970.
  2643.   Poems.   Norwood, PA: Telegraph Books, 1972.
  2644.   The rest.   Norwood, PA: Telegraph Books, 1973.

SARTON, May
  2645.   Encounter in April.   Boston: Houghton Mifflin, 1936.
  2646.   Inner landscape.   Boston: Houghton Mifflin, 1939.
  2647.   The lion and the rose.   New York: Rinehart, 1948.
  2648.   The land of silence, and other poems.   New York:
             Rinehart, 1953.
  2649.   In time like air.   New York: Rinehart, 1958.
  2650.   Cloud stone sun vine.   New York: Norton, 1961.
  2651.   A private mythology; new poems.   New York: Norton,
             1966.
  2652.   As does New Hampshire, and other poems.   Peter-
             borough, NH: R. R. Smith, 1967.
  2653.   A grain of mustard seed; new poems.   New York:
             Norton, 1971.
  2654.   A durable fire; new poems.   New York: Norton, 1972.

SAVORY, Teo
  2655.   Traveler's palm; a poetry sequence.   Santa Barbara:
             Unicorn, 1967.
  2656.   Snow vole: a poetry sequence.   Santa Barbara: Uni-
             corn, 1968.
  2657.   To a high place.   Santa Barbara: Unicorn, 1971.
  2658.   Transitions.   Santa Barbara: Unicorn, 1973.

SCARBROUGH, George
  2659.   The course is upward.   New York: Dutton, 1951.

2660.   Summer so-called.   New York: Dutton, 1956.

SCHAFF, David
    2661.   The moon by day.   San Francisco: Four Seasons, 1971.

SCHECHTER, Ruth Lisa
    2662.   Suddenly thunder.   New York: Barlenmir House, 1972.

SCHEVILL, James
    2663.   Tensions.   Berkeley: Gillick, 1947.
    2664.   The American fantasies.   Agana, Guam: Bern Porter,
            1951.
    2665.   The right to greet.   San Francisco: Bern Porter, 1955.
    2666.   Selected poems, 1945-1959.   n.p., Bern Porter, 1960.
    2667.   Private dooms and public destinations; poems, 1945-
            1962.   Denver: Swallow, 1962.
    2668.   The Stalingrad elegies.   Denver: Swallow, 1964.
    2669.   Release.   Providence, RI: Hellcoal, 1968.
    2670.   Violence and glory: poems, 1962-1968.   Chicago:
            Swallow, 1969.
    2671.   The Buddhist car and other characters.   Chicago:
            Swallow, 1973.

SCHIFF, Harris
    2672.   Secret clouds.   New York: Angel Hair, 1970.

SCHJELDAHL, Peter
    2673.   White country.   New York: Corinth, 1968.
    2674.   An adventure of the thought police.   London: Ferry
            Press, 1971.
    2675.   Dreams.   New York: Angel Hair, 1973.

SCHMITZ, Dennis
    2676.   We weep for our strangeness.   Chicago: Big Table,
            1969.

SCHONBORG, Virginia
    2677.   The salt marsh.   New York: Morrow, 1969.
    2678.   Subway swinger.   New York: Morrow, 1970.

SCHRAMM, Richard
    2679.   Rooted in silence.   Indianapolis: Bobbs-Merrill, 1972.

SCHUBERT, David
    2680.   Initial A; a book of poems.   New York: Macmillan,
            1961.

SCHUYLER, James
    2681.   Salute.   New York: Tiber, 1960.
    2682.   May 24th or so.   New York: Tibor de Nagy, 1966.
    2683.   Freely espousing.   Garden City, NY: Doubleday, 1969.
    2684.   Verge.   New York: Angel Hair, 1971.
    2685.   The crystal lithium.   New York: Random House, 1972.

SCHWARTZ, Barry
  2686. The voyeur of our time. New York: Barlenmir House,
          1973.

SCHWARTZ, Delmore
  2687. In dreams begin responsibilities. Norfolk, CT: New
          Directions, 1938.
  2688. Shenandoah. Norfolk, CT: New Directions, 1941.
  2689. Genesis I. Norfolk, CT: New Directions, 1943.
  2690. Vaudeville for a princess, and other poems. New
          York: New Directions, 1950.
  2691. Summer knowledge; new and selected poems, 1938-1958.
          Garden City, NY: Doubleday, 1959.

SCHWERNER, Armand
  2692. The lightfall. New York: Hawk's Well, 1964.
  2693. If personal; window poem. Los Angeles: Black Spar-
          row, 1968.
  2694. Seaweed. Los Angeles: Black Sparrow, 1969.
  2695. The tablets. Cummington, MA: Cummington, 1969.
  2696. The tablets I-XV. New York: Grossman, 1971.

SCOTT, Dennis
  2697. Uncle time. Pittsburgh: University of Pittsburgh
          Press, 1973.

SCOTT, Winfield Townley
  2698. The dark sister. New York: New York University
          Press, 1958.
  2699. Scrimshaw. New York: Macmillan, 1959.
  2700. Change of weather. Garden City, NY: Doubleday,
          1964.
  2701. Collected poems, 1937-1962. New York: Macmillan,
          1962.
  2702. New and selected poems. Garden City, NY: Double-
          day, 1967.

SCOTT-HERON, Gil
  2703. Small talk at 125th and Lenox; a collection of Black
          poems. New York: World, 1970.
  2704. The nigger factory. New York: Dial, 1972.

SCULLY, James
  2705. The marches; a book of poems. New York: Holt,
          Rinehart and Winston, 1967.
  2706. Avenue of the Americas. Amherst: University of
          Massachusetts Press, 1971.

SEALEY, Danguole
  2707. Recollections of a childhood. New York: Manyland,
          1971.
  2708. Let not your hart. Middletown, CT: Wesleyan Univer-
          sity Press, 1970.

SEBENTHALL, R. E.
  2709. Acquainted with a chance of bobcats. New Brunswick,
          NJ: Rutgers University Press, 1969.
  2710. The cold ones. New York: Simon and Schuster, 1972.

SEIDEL, Frederick
  2711. Final solutions. New York: Random House, 1963.

SEIDMAN, Hugh
  2712. Collecting evidence. New Haven: Yale University
          Press, 1970.

SEWELL, Elizabeth
  2713. Poems, 1947-1961. Chapel Hill: University of North
          Carolina Press, 1962.
  2714. Signs and cities. Chapel Hill: University of North
          Carolina Press, 1968.

SEXTON, Anne
  2715. To Bedlam and part way back. Boston: Houghton Mif-
          flin, 1960.
  2716. All my pretty ones. Boston: Houghton Mifflin, 1962.
  2717. Selected poems. New York and London: Oxford Uni-
          versity Press, 1964.
  2718. Live or die. Boston: Houghton Mifflin, 1966.
  2719. Love poems. Boston: Houghton Mifflin, 1969.
  2720. Transformations. Boston: Houghton Mifflin, 1971;
          London: Oxford University Press, 1972.
  2721. The book of folly. Boston: Houghton Mifflin, 1972.

SHAPIRO, David
  2722. January; a book of poems. New York: Holt, Rinehart
          and Winston, 1965.
  2723. Poems from Deal. New York: Dutton, 1969.
  2724. A man holding an acoustic panel. New York: Dutton,
          1971.
  2725. The page turner. New York: Liveright, 1973.

SHAPIRO, Harvey
  2726. The eye. Denver: Swallow, 1953.
  2727. The book, and other poems. Rowe, MA: Cummington,
          1955.
  2728. Mountain, fire, thornbush. Denver: Swallow, 1961.
  2729. Battle report; selected poems. Middletown, CT:
          Wesleyan University Press, 1966.
  2730. This world. Middletown, CT: Wesleyan University
          Press, 1971.

SHAPIRO, Karl
  2731. Poems. Baltimore: Waverly, 1935.
  2732. Person, place, and thing. New York: Reynal and
          Hitchcock, 1942; London: Secker and Warburg, 1944.
  2733. The place of love. Malvern, Australia: Bradley

Printers, 1942.
2734. V-Letter and other poems. New York: Reynal and
       Hitchcock, 1944; London: Secker and Warburg, 1945.
2735. Essay on rime. New York: Reynal and Hitchcock,
       1945; London: Secker and Warburg, 1947.
2736. Trial of a poet. New York: Reynal and Hitchcock,
       1947.
2737. Poems, 1940-1953. New York: Random House, 1953.
2738. Poems of a Jew. New York: Random House, 1958.
2739. The bourgeois poet. New York: Random House, 1964.
2740. Selected poems. New York: Random House, 1968.
2741. White-haired lover. New York: Random House, 1968.

SHATTUCK, Roger
2742. Half tame. Austin: University of Texas Press, 1964.

SHELTON, Richard
2743. Journal of return. Santa Cruz, CA: Kayak, 1968.
2744. The tattooed desert. Pittsburgh: University of Pitts-
       burgh Press, 1971.
2745. Calendar: a cycle of poems. Phoenix: Baleen, 1972.
2746. The heroes of our time. Crete, NE: Best Cellar,
       1972.
2747. Of all the dirty words. Pittsburgh: University of
       Pittsburgh Press, 1972.

SHEPARD, Lucius
2748. Cantata of death, weakmind & generation. Chapel Hill,
       NC: Lillabulero, 1967.

SHERWIN, Judith Johnson
2749. Uranium poems. New Haven: Yale University Press,
       1969.
2750. Impossible buildings. Garden City, NY: Doubleday,
       1973.

SHIFFERT, Edith
2751. In open woods. Denver: Swallow, 1961.
2752. For a return to Kona: island poems. Denver: Swal-
       low, 1964.

SHOEMAKER, Lynn
2753. Coming home. Ithaca, NY: Ithaca House, 1973.

SHRADER, Stephen
2754. Leaving by the closet door. Ithaca, NY: Ithaca
       House, 1970.

SIEGEL, Eli
2755. Hot afternoons have been in Montana. New York:
       Definition, 1957.
2756. Hail, American development. New York: Definition,
       1968.

SILLIMAN, Ronald
2757. Crow. Ithaca, NY: Ithaca House, 1971.

SIMIC, Charles
2758. What the grass says. Santa Cruz, CA: Kayak, 1966.
2759. Somewhere among us a stone is taking notes. Santa Cruz, CA: Kayak, 1968.
2760. Dismantling the silence. New York: Braziller, and London: Cape, 1971.
2761. White by Simic. New York: New Rivers, 1972.

SIMMONS, Edgar
2762. Driving to Biloxi. Baton Rouge: Louisiana State University Press, 1968.

SIMMONS, J. D.
2763. Judith's blues. Detroit: Broadside, 1973.

SIMON, John Oliver
2764. Adventures of a floating rabbi. Sacramento: Runcible Spoon, 1968.
2765. Roads to Dawn Lake. Berkeley: Oyez, 1968.

SIMPSON, Louis
2766. The arrivistes. New York: Fine Editions, 1949.
2767. Good news of death. New York: Scribner, 1955.
2768. A dream of governors. Middletown, CT: Wesleyan University Press, 1959.
2769. At the end of the open road. Middletown, CT: Wesleyan University Press, 1963.
2770. Selected poems. New York: Harcourt, Brace, 1965.
2771. Adventures of the letter I. New York: Harper & Row, 1971.
2772. North of Jamaica. New York: Harper & Row, 1972.

SISSMAN, L. E.
2773. Dying, an introduction. Boston: Little, Brown, 1968.
2774. Scattered returns. Boston: Little, Brown, 1969.
2775. Pursuit of honor. Boston: Little, Brown, 1971.

SKELTON, Robin
2776. A different mountain. Santa Cruz, CA: Kayak, 1970.

SLAVITT, David R.
2777. Suits for the dead. New York: Scribner, 1961.
2778. The carnivore. Chapel Hill: University of North Carolina Press, 1965.
2779. Day sailing. Chapel Hill: University of North Carolina Press, 1969.
2780. Child's play. Baton Rouge: Louisiana State University Press, 1972.

113   Slesinger

SLESINGER, Warren
2781. Field with figurations. Iowa City: Cummington, 1970.

SLOMAN, Joel
2782. Virgil's machines. New York: Norton, 1966.

SMITH, LeRoy
2783. The fourth king. New York: Macmillan, 1953.
2784. A character invented. New York: Macmillan, 1954.
2785. The opulent citizen. New York: Macmillan, 1957.

SMITH, Patti
2786. Seventh heaven. Norwood, PA: Telegraph Books, 1973.

SMITH, Ray
2787. The deer on the freeway. Vermillion: University of
       South Dakota Press, 1973.

SMITH, William Jay
2788. Poems. Pawlet, VT: Banyan, 1947.
2789. Celebration at dark. New York: Farrar, Straus, 1950.
2790. Poems: 1947-1957. Boston: Little, Brown, 1957.
2791. The tin can, and other poems. New York: Delacorte,
       1966.
2792. Mr. Smith & other nonsense. New York: Delacorte,
       1968.
2793. New & selected poems. New York: Delacorte, 1970.

SNODGRASS, W. D.
2794. Heart's needle. New York: Knopf, 1959; Hessle, Eng.:
       Marvell, 1960.
2795. After experience. New York: Harper & Row, 1968;
       London: Oxford University Press, 1969.
2796. Remains; poems by S. S. Gardons. Mt. Horeb, WI:
       Perishable Press, 1970.

SNYDER, Gary
2797. Riprap. Ashland, MA: Origin, 1959.
2798. Myths & texts. New York: Totem, 1960.
2799. The firing. R. L. Ross, 1964.
2800. Hop, skip, and jump. Berkeley: Oyez, 1964.
2801. Nanoa knows. San Francisco: Four Seasons, 1964.
2802. Riprap & Cold Mountain poems. San Francisco: Four
       Seasons, 1965.
2803. Six sections from Mountains and rivers without end.
       San Francisco: Four Seasons, 1965; London: Ful-
       crum, 1967.
2804. A range of poems. London: Fulcrum, 1966.
2805. The back country. London: Fulcrum, 1967; New York:
       New Directions, 1968.
2806. Regarding wave. Iowa City: Windhover, 1969; rev.
       enl. New York: New Directions, 1970; London: Ful-
       crum, 1972.

2807. Fudo trilogy. Berkeley: Shaman Drum, 1972.
2808. Manzantu. San Francisco: Four Seasons, 1972.

SNYDER, Richard
2809. A keeping in touch. Ashland, OH: Ashland Poetry
       Press, 1970.

SOBILOFF, Hy
2810. When children played as kings and queens. Privately
       printed, 1948.
2811. Dinosaurs and violins. New York: Farrar, Straus,
       1954.
2812. In the deepest aquarium. New York: Dial, 1959.
2813. Breathing of first things. New York: Dial, 1963.
2814. Hooting across the silence. New York: Horizon, 1971.

SORRELLS, Helen
2815. Seeds as they fall. Nashville: Vanderbilt University
       Press, 1971.

SORRENTINO, Gilbert
2816. The darkness surrounds us. Highlands, NC: J. Wil-
       liams, 1960.
2817. Black and white. New York: Totem, 1964.
2818. The perfect fiction. New York: Norton, 1968.
2819. Steelwork. Los Angeles: Pantheon, 1970.
2820. Corrosive sublimate. Los Angeles: Black Sparrow,
       1971.
2821. Imaginative qualities of actual things. Los Angeles:
       Pantheon, 1972.
2822. Splendite-Hôtel. New York: New Directions, 1973.

SPACKS, Barry
2823. The company of children. Garden City, NY: Double-
       day, 1968.
2824. Something human. New York: Harper's Magazine,
       1972.

SPELLMAN, Alfred
2825. The beautiful day and others. New York: Poets Press,
       1964.

SPICER, Jack
2826. Language. San Francisco: White Rabbit, 1965.
2827. Book of magazine verse. Santa Barbara: White Rab-
       bit/Open Space, 1966.
2828. The holy grail. Cambridge, MA: Augtwofive, 1970.

SPIVACK, Kathleen
2829. Flying inland. Garden City, NY: Doubleday, 1973.

SQUIRES, James Radcliffe
2830. Where the compass spins. New York: Twayne, 1951.

2831. Fingers of Hermes. Ann Arbor: University of Michigan Press, 1965.
2832. The light under islands. Ann Arbor: University of Michigan Press, 1967.

STAFFORD, William
2833. Winterward. Ann Arbor: University Microfilms, 1954.
2834. West of your city. Georgetown, CA: Talisman, 1960.
2835. Traveling through the dark. New York: Harper & Row, 1962.
2836. The rescued year. New York: Harper & Row, 1966.
2837. William Stafford: eleven untitled poems. Mt. Horeb, WI: Perishable Press, 1968.
2838. Weather. Mt. Horeb, WI: Perishable Press, 1969.
2839. Allegiances. New York: Harper & Row, 1970.
2840. Temporary facts. Athens, OH: D. Schneider, 1970.
2841. Someday, maybe. New York: Harper & Row, 1973.

STANFORD, Ann
2842. In narrow bound. Denver: Swallow, 1943.
2843. The white bird. Denver: Swallow, 1949.
2844. Magellan: a poem to be read by several voices. San Jose, CA: Talisman, 1958.
2845. The weathercock. New York: Viking, 1966.
2846. The descent. New York: Viking, 1970.

STANLEY, George
2847. The love root. San Francisco: White Rabbit, 1958.
2848. Beyond love. San Francisco: Open Space/Dariel, 1968.
2849. Tete rouge/pony express riders. San Francisco: White Rabbit, 1963.
2850. Flowers. San Francisco: White Rabbit, 1965.
2851. You. San Francisco: Four Seasons, 1971.

STAPLETON, Laurence
2852. Yushin's log and other poems. New York: A. S. Barnes, 1969.

STARBUCK, George
2853. Bone thoughts. New Haven: Yale University Press, 1960.
2854. White paper. Boston: Little, Brown, 1966.

STEFANILE, Felix
2855. A fig tree/in America. New Rochelle, NY: Elizabeth, 1970.

STEIN, Charles
2856. The virgo poem. New York: Angel Hair, 1967.

STEINGASS, David
2857. Body compass. Pittsburgh: University of Pittsburgh Press, 1969.

2858. American handbook. Pittsburgh: University of Pitts-
burgh Press, 1973.

STEPANCHEV, Stephen
2859. Three priests in April. Baltimore: Contemporary
Poetry, 1956.
2860. Spring in the harbor. Flushing, NY: Amity, 1967.
2861. A man running in the rain. Los Angeles: Black Spar-
row, 1969.
2862. The mad bomber. Los Angeles: Black Sparrow, 1972.
2863. [no entry]

STEPHENS, Alan
2864. The sum. Denver: Swallow, 1958.
2865. Between matter and principle. Denver: Swallow, 1963.
2866. The heat lightning. Brunswick, ME: Bowdoin College
Museum of Art, 1967.
2867. Tree meditation, and others. Chicago: Swallow, 1970.

STERN, Gerald
2868. The naming of beasts. Iowa City: Cummington, 1973.

STERN, Gerd
2869. Afterimage. Woodstock, NY: Maverick, 1966.

STEVENSON, Anne
2870. Reversals. Middletown, CT: Wesleyan University
Press, 1969.

STEVENSON, Wade
2871. Beds. New York: McCall, 1970.

STOKES, Terry
2872. Balancing-out. Sacramento: Runcible Spoon, 1968.
2873. The lady poems. Sacramento: Runcible Spoon, 1969.
2874. The satanic American flag. Glen Ellyn, IL: Two Bags,
1970.
2875. Natural disasters. New York: New York University
Press, 1971.
2876. Crimes of passion. New York: Knopf, 1973.
2877. Punching in, punching out. Providence, RI: Burning
Deck, 1973.

STOLOFF, Carolyn
2878. Triptych. Santa Barbara: Unicorn, 1970.
2879. Stepping out. Greensboro, NC: Unicorn, 1971.
2880. Dying to survive. Garden City, NY: Doubleday, 1973.

STONE, John
2881. The smell of matches. New Brunswick, NJ: Rutgers
University Press, 1972.

STONE, Ruth
    2882. In an iridescent time. New York: Harcourt, Brace, 1959.
    2883. Topography, and other poems. New York: Harcourt, Brace, 1971.

STOREY, Edward
    2884. A man in winter. Middletown, CT: Wesleyan University Press, 1973.

STORM, Hester G.
    2885. Wrongside-up rainbow. Denver: Swallow, 1964.

STOUTENBURG, Adrien (see also KENDALL, Lace)
    2886. Short history of the fur trade. Boston: Houghton Mifflin, 1969; London: Deutsch, 1970.

STOWERS, J. Anthony
    2887. The aliens. San Francisco: White Rabbit, 1967.

STRAND, Mark
    2888. Sleeping with one eye open. Iowa City: Stone Wall, 1964.
    2889. Reasons for moving. New York: Atheneum, 1968.
    2890. Darker. New York: Atheneum, 1970.
    2891. 18 poems from the Quechua. Cambridge, MA: H. Ferguson, 1971.
    2892. The Sargentville notebook. Providence, RI: Burning Deck, 1973.
    2893. The story of our lives. New York: Atheneum, 1973.

STRYK, Lucien
    2894. Taproot. Oxford: Fantasy, 1953.
    2895. The trespasser. Oxford: Fantasy, 1956.
    2896. Notes for a guidebook. Denver: Swallow, 1965.
    2897. The pit and other poems. Chicago: Swallow, 1969.
    2898. Awakening. Chicago: Swallow, 1973.

STUART, Dabney
    2899. The diving bell. New York: Knopf, 1966.
    2900. A particular place. New York: Knopf, 1969.

SULLIVAN, May M.
    2901. Not that far. San Luis Obispo, CA: Solo, 1972.

SULLIVAN, Nancy
    2902. The history of the world as pictures. Columbia: University of Missouri Press, 1965.

SUMMERS, Hollis
    2903. The walks near Athens. New York: Harper, 1959.
    2904. Someone else. Philadelphia: Lippincott, 1962.
    2905. Seven occasions. New Brunswick, NJ: Rutgers

University Press, 1964.
2906. The peddler and other domestic matters. New Bruns-
        wick, NJ: Rutgers University Press, 1967.
2907. Sit opposite each other. New Brunswick, NJ: Rutgers
        University Press, 1970.
2908. Start from home. New Brunswick, NJ: Rutgers Uni-
        versity Press, 1972.

SUND, Robert
2909. Bunch grass. Seattle: University of Washington Press,
        1969.

SUSLICK, Edith
2910. Interstices. Madison, WI: Abraxas, 1970.

SWALLOW, Alan
2911. The nameless sight; poems, 1937-1956. Iowa City:
        Prairie Press, 1956.

SWAN, Jon
2912. Journeys and return. New York: Scribner, 1960.

SWARD, Robert
2913. Advertisements. Chicago: Odyssey Chapbook, 1958.
2914. Uncle dog. London: Putnam, 1962.
2915. Kissing the dancer & other poems. Ithaca, NY:
        Cornell University Press, 1964.
2916. Thousand-year-old fiancée, & other poems. Ithaca,
        NY: Cornell University Press, 1965.
2917. In Mexico. London: Ambit, 1966.
2918. Horgbortom Stringbottom I am yours, you are history.
        Chicago: Swallow, 1970.
2919. Poems: new and selected (1957-1973) Half-a-life's his-
        tory. Chicago: Swallow, 1973.

SWENSON, May
2920. Another animal. New York: Scribner, 1954.
2921. A cage of spines. New York: Rinehart, 1958.
2922. To mix with time, new and selected poems. New York:
        Scribner, 1963.
2923. Poems to solve. New York: Scribner, 1966.
2924. Half sun, half sleep; new poems. New York: Scribner,
        1967.
2925. Iconographs. New York: Scribner, 1970.
2926. More poems to solve. New York: Scribner, 1971.

SWIFT, Joan
2927. This element. Denver: Swallow, 1965.

SWOBODA, George
2928. Sideshow. Madison, WI: Abraxas, 1969.

TAGGART, John
    2929. To construct a clock. New Rochelle, NY: Elizabeth,
           1971.

TAGLIABUE, John
    2930. Poems. New York: Harper, 1959.
    2931. A Japanese journal. San Francisco: Kayak, 1966.
    2932. The Buddha uproar. San Francisco: Kayak, 1967.
    2933. The doorless door (Japan poems). New York: Gross-
           man, 1970.

TALARICO, Ross
    2934. Snowfires. Crete, NE: Best Cellar, 1972.

TARGAN, Barry
    2935. Let the wild rumpus start. Crete, NE: Best Cellar,
           1971.

TARN, Nathaniel
    2936. The beautiful contradictions. New York: Goliard/
           Grossman, 1970.

TATE, James
    2937. Cages. Iowa City: Shepherds, 1967.
    2938. The destination. Cambridge, MA: Pym-Randall, 1967.
    2939. The lost pilot. New Haven: Yale University Press,
           1967.
    2940. Camping in the valley. Chicago: Madison Park, 1968.
    2941. Mystics in Chicago. Santa Barbara: Unicorn, 1968.
    2942. Notes of woe. Iowa City: Stone Wall, 1968.
    2943. Is there anything. Fremont, MI: Sumac, 1969.
    2944. Row with your hair. San Francisco: Kayak, 1969.
    2945. Shepherds of the mist. Los Angeles: Black Sparrow,
           1969.
    2946. Amnesia people. Pittsburg, KA: Little Balkans, 1970.
    2947. Deaf girl playing. Cambridge, MA: Pym-Randall,
           1970.
    2948. The oblivion ha-ha; sixty poems. Boston: Little,
           Brown, 1970.
    2949. Wrong songs. Cambridge, MA: Ferguson, 1970.
    2950. Hints to pilgrims. Cambridge, MA: Ferguson, 1971.
    2951. The torches. Los Angeles: Black Sparrow, 1971.
    2952. Absences; new poems. Boston: Little, Brown, 1972.
    2953. Apology for eating Geoffrey Movius' hyacinth. Los
           Angeles: Black Sparrow, 1972.

TAYLOR, Eleanor Ross
    2954. Wilderness of ladies. New York: McDowell, Obolensky,
           1960.
    2955. Welcome Eumenides. New York: Braziller, 1972.

TAYLOR, Henry
    2956. The horse show at midnight. Baton Rouge: Louisiana

State University Press, 1966.
2957. Breakings. San Luis Obispo, CA: Solo, 1971.

TAYLOR, Rod
2958. Florida east coast champion. San Francisco: Straight
Arrow, 1972.

THAYLER, Carl
2959. The providings. Fremont, MI: Sumac, 1971.

THIBEAU, Jack
2960. Conversations with Apollinaire. Santa Barbara: White
Rabbit/Open Space, 1972.

THIGPEN, William A.
2961. Down Nigger paved streets. Detroit: Broadside, 1972.

THOMAS, Lorenzo
2962. Fit music. New York: Angel Hair, 1972.
2963. Dracula. New York: Angel Hair, 1973.

THOMPSON, Carolyn
2964. Frank. Detroit: Broadside, 1970.

THOMPSON, James W.
2965. First fire: poems, 1957-1960. London: Breman,
1970.

THOMPSON, Phyllis
2966. Artichoke & other poems. Honolulu: University of
Hawaii Press, 1969.
2967. Creation frame. Urbana: University of Illinois Press,
1974.

THOMSON, Derick
2968. The far road. New York: New Rivers, 1972.

THORNE, Evelyn
2969. Answer in bright green. Crescent City, FL: New
Athenaeum, 1968.
2970. Ways of listening. Homestead, FL: Olivant, 1969.

TILLINGHAST, Richard
2971. Sleep watch. Middletown, CT: Wesleyan University
Press, 1969.

TIPTON, James
2972. Stump farming. Santa Barbara: Unicorn, 1972.

TOLSON, Melvin
2973. Rendezvous with America. New York: Dodd, Mead,
1944.
2974. Libretto for the Republic of Liberia. New York:

Twayne, 1953.
2975. Harlem gallery. New York: Twayne, 1965.

TORGERSEN, Eric
2976. At war with friends. Ithaca, NY: Ithaca House, 1972.

TORREGIAN, Sotère
2977. Song for woman. Joycian Ct., 1966.
2978. The golden palomino bites the clock. New York:
   Angel Hair, 1967.
2979. The wounded mattress. Berkeley: Oyez, 1971.

TOUSTER, Saul
2980. Still lives and other lives. Columbia: University of
   Missouri Press, 1966.

TOWLE, Tony
2981. Poems. New York: privately printed, 1966.
2982. After dinner we take a drive into the night. New York:
   Tibor de Nagy, 1968.
2983. North. New York: Columbia University Press, 1970.

TREMBLAY, Bill
2984. Crying in the cheap seats. Amherst: University of
   Massachusetts Press, 1971.

TRIMPI, Wesley
2985. The glass of Perseus. Denver: Swallow, 1953.

TROUPE, Quincy
2986. Embryo. New York: Barlenmir House, 1972.

TRUDELL, Dennis
2987. Avenues. Crete, NE: Best Cellar, 1972.

TURCO, Lewis
2988. Day after history; a selection of poems. Arlington,
   VA, 1956.
2989. First poems. Francestown, NH: Golden Quill, 1960.
2990. The sketches of Lewis Turco and Livevil: a mask.
   Cleveland: American Weave, 1962.
2991. Awaken, bells falling; poems 1959-1967. Columbia:
   University of Missouri Press, 1968.
2992. The inhabitant. Northampton, MA: Despa, 1970.
2993. Pocoangelini: a fantography, and other poems. North-
   ampton, MA: Despa, 1971.
2994. The weed garden. Orangeburg, SC: Peaceweed, 1973.

TURNER, Alberta T.
2995. Need. Ashland, Ohio: Ashland Poetry Press, 1971.

TURNER, Fred
2996. Deep-sea fish. Santa Barbara: Unicorn, 1968.

2997. Between two lives. Middletown, CT: Wesleyan University Press, 1972.

TUSIANI, Joseph
2998. Rind and all; fifty poems. New York: Monastine Press, 1962.
2999. The fifth season. New York: I. Obolensky, 1964.

TYLER, Parker
3000. The metaphor in the jungle. Prairie City, IL: Decker, 1940.
3001. The granite butterfly. Sauselito, CA: Bern Porter, 1945.
3002. Yesterday's children. New York: Harper, 1947.
3003. The will of Eros; selected poems 1930-1970. Los Angeles: Black Sparrow, 1972.

TYSH, George
3004. A knot of noodles. Detroit: Alternative, 1970.
3005. Shop posh. Providence, RI: Burning Deck, 1973.

UNTERECKER, John
3006. The dreaming zoo. New York: Henry Z. Walk, 1965.
3007. Irish poems. Dublin: Dolmen, 1973.

UPDIKE, John
3008. The carpentered hen and other tame creatures. New York: Harper, 1958; [as] Hoping for a hoopoe. London: Gollancz, 1959.
3009. Telephone poles, and other poems. New York: Knopf, and London: Deutsch, 1963.
3010. The angels. Pensacola, FL: King & Queen Press, 1968.
3011. Midpoint, and other poems. New York: Knopf, and London: Deutsch, 1969.
3012. The dance of the solids. Ipswich, MA, 1969.

UPTON, Charles
3013. Panic grass. San Francisco: City Lights, 1968.
3014. Time raid. San Francisco: Four Seasons, 1969.

URDANG, Constance
3015. Charades and celebrations. New York: October House, 1965.
3016. Natural history. New York: Harper & Row, 1969.

URONOVITZ, B. A.
3017. Reflections in the dark. New Rochelle, NY: Elizabeth, 1961.

VALENS, E. G.
    3018. Cybernaut; a space poem. New York: Viking, 1968.

VALENTINE, Jean
    3019. Dream barker, and other poems. New Haven: Yale
          University Press, 1965.
    3020. Pilgrims. New York: Farrar, Straus, 1969.

VAN BRUNT, H. L.
    3021. Uncertainties. New York: The Smith, 1968.
    3022. Indian territory and other poems. New York: The
          Smith, 1974.

VANCE, Thomas
    3023. Skeleton of light. Chapel Hill: University of North
          Carolina Press, 1961.

VANDERBILT, Gloria
    3024. Love poems. Cleveland: World, 1955.

VANDER MOLEN, Robert
    3025. Blood ink. East Lansing, MI: Zeitgeist, 1967.
    3026. Variations. East Lansing, MI: Zeitgeist, 1970.
    3027. The invisible lost book of deep ocean fish. East Lans-
          ing, MI: Zeitgeist, 1970.

VAN DUYN, Mona
    3028. Valentines to the wide world. Cummington, MA: Cum-
          mington, 1958.
    3029. A time of bees. Chapel Hill: University of North
          Carolina Press, 1964.
    3030. To see, to take. New York: Atheneum, 1970.
    3031. Merciful disguises. New York: Atheneum, 1973.

VAS DIAS, Robert
    3032. Ribbed vision. New York: privately printed, 1963.
    3033. The counted. New York: Caterpillar, 1967.
    3034. Written, in orbit. New York: Pierrepont, 1970.
    3035. Speech acts & happenings. Indianapolis: Bobbs-Merrill,
          1972.

VASQUEZ, Richard
    3036. Chicano. Garden City, NY: Doubleday, 1971.

VAZAKAS, Byron
    3037. The equal tribunals. New York: Clarke and Way,
          1962.
    3038. The marble manifesto. New York: October House,
          1966.
    3039. Nostalgias for a house of cards. New York: October
          House, 1970.

VEITCH, Tom (see also PADGETT, Ron)
3040. Cooked zeros. Stinson Beach, CA: Grape, 1970.

VERMONT, Charlie
3041. Two women. New York: Angel Hair, 1971.

VESEY, Paul see ALLEN, Samuel W.

VIERECK, Peter
3042. Terror and decorum. New York: Scribner, 1948.
3043. Strike through the mask! New York: Scribner, 1950.
3044. The first morning, new poems. New York: Scribner, 1952.
3045. The persimmon tree; new pastoral and lyrical poems. New York: Scribner, 1956.
3046. The tree witch. New York: Scribner, 1961.
3047. New and selected poems, 1932-1967. Indianapolis: Bobbs-Merrill, 1967.

VILLA, José Garcia
3048. Selected poems and new. New York: McDowell, Obolensky, 1958.
3049. Poems in praise of love. Manila: A. S. Florentino, 1962.
3050. The essential Villa. Detroit: Cellar Book, 1965.

VINCENT, Stephen
3051. White lights and whale hearts. Trumansburg, NY: Crossing Press, 1971.

VINOGRAD, Julia
3052. Revolution, and other poems. Berkeley: Oyez, 1970.
3053. The Berkeley bead game. Berkeley: Cody's Books, 1971.

VIOLI, Paul
3054. Automatic transmission. New York: Kulchur, 1973.
3055. Waterworks. West Branch, IA: Toothpaste, 1973.

VIORST, Judith
3056. The village square. New York: Coward-McCann, 1966.
3057. It's hard to be hip over thirty, and other tragedies of married life. New York: World, 1968.
3058. Try it again, Sam: safety when you walk. Lothrop, 1970.
3059. People & other aggravations. New York: World, 1971.
3060. [no entry]

VLIET, R. G.
3061. Sand is the tool. New York: William-Frederick, 1953.
3062. Events & celebrations. New York: Viking, 1966.
3063. The man with the black mouth. Santa Cruz, CA: Kayak, 1970.

WADE, John S.
  3064. Gallery. London: Poet and Printer, 1970.
  3065. Cats in the colosseum. Trumansburg, NY: Crossing
        Press, 1972.

WAGNER, d. r.
  3066. Book for Barb. Berkeley: Undermine, 1967.
  3067. At rest in the fields. Sacramento: Grande Ronde,
        1968.
  3068. The footsteps of the returning king. Sacramento:
        Runcible Spoon, 1968.
  3069. Four dream leaves & dreamers of the land. Sacramen-
        to: Runcible Spoon, 1968.
  3070. Plump poon poems & slumped slit songs. Sacramento:
        Runcible Spoon, n. d.
  3071. Putah Creek overflow. Sacramento: Runcible Spoon,
        1968.
  3072. The union camp papers. San Francisco: Twowindows,
        1968.

WAGONER, David
  3073. Dry sun, dry wind. Bloomington: Indiana University
        Press, 1953.
  3074. A place to stand. Bloomington: Indiana University
        Press, 1958.
  3075. The nesting ground, a book of poems. Bloomington:
        Indiana University Press, 1963.
  3076. Staying alive. Bloomington: Indiana University Press,
        1966.
  3077. New and selected poems. Bloomington: Indiana Uni-
        versity Press, 1969.
  3078. Working against time. London: Rapp & Whiting, 1970.
  3079. Riverbed. Bloomington: Indiana University Press,
        1972.

WAHLE, F. Keith
  3080. The part-time arsonist. Madison, WI: Abraxas, 1971.

WAKOSKI, Diane
  3081. Coins and coffins. New York: Hawk's Well, 1962.
  3082. Discrepancies and apparitions. Garden City, NY:
        Doubleday, 1966.
  3083. The George Washington poems. New York: Riverrun,
        1967.
  3084. The diamond merchant. Cambridge, MA: Sans Souci,
        1968.
  3085. Greed; parts 1 & 2. Los Angeles: Black Sparrow,
        1968; rev. enl., 1971.
  3086. Inside the blood factory. Garden City, NY: Doubleday,
        1968.
  3087. The moon has a complicated geography. San Francisco:
        Odda Tala, 1969.
  3088. Some poems for Buddha's birthday. New York:

Pierrepont, 1969.
3089. Thanking my mother for piano lessons.   Mt. Horeb,
      WI: Perishable Press, 1969.
3090. Black dream ditty for Billy "the Kid" M seen in Dr.
      Generosity's bar recruiting for Hell's Angels and
      Black Mafia.   Los Angeles: Black Sparrow, 1970.
3091. The Magellanic clouds.   Los Angeles: Black Sparrow,
      1970.
3092. Greed, parts 5-7.   Los Angeles: Black Sparrow, 1971.
3093. The motorcycle betrayal poems.   New York: Simon
      and Schuster, 1971.
3094. On Barbara's shore.   Los Angeles: Black Sparrow,
      1971.
3095. Smudging.   Los Angeles: Black Sparrow, 1972.
3096. Greed, parts 8, 9 & 11.   Los Angeles: Black Sparrow:
      1973.
3097. The pumpkin pie.   Los Angeles: Black Sparrow, 1973.
3098. Sometimes a poet will hijack the moon.   Providence,
      RI: Burning Deck, 1973.

WALDMAN, Anne
3099. Oh my life! New York: Angel Hair, 1969.
3100. Up through the years.   New York: Angel Hair, 1969.
3101. Baby breakdown.   Indianapolis: Bobbs-Merrill, 1970.
3102. Giant night.   New York: Corinth, 1970.
3103. No hassles.   New York: Corinth, 1970.
3104. Icy rose.   New York: Angel Hair, 1971.
3105. Life notes.   Indianapolis: Bobbs-Merrill, 1973.

WALDROP, Keith
3106. A windmill near Calvary.   Ann Arbor: University of
      Michigan Press, 1968.
3107. The Antichrist and other foundlings.   Providence, RI:
      Burning Deck, 1970.
3108. To the sincere reader.   New York: Wittenborn, 1971.

WALDROP, Rosemarie
3109. The relaxed abalone; or, what-you-may-find.   Provi-
      dence, RI: Burning Deck, 1970.
3110. The aggressive ways of the casual stranger.   New York:
      Random House, 1972.

WALKER, Alice
3111. Once.   New York: Harcourt, Brace, 1968.
3112. Revolutionary petunias.   New York: Harcourt, Brace,
      1973.

WALKER, Margaret
3113. Ballad of the free.   Detroit: Broadside, 1966.
3114. For my people.   New York: Arno, 1968.
3115. Prophets for a new day.   Detroit: Broadside, 1970.
3116. October journey.   Detroit: Broadside, 1973.

WALLACE, Robert
3117. Views from a ferris wheel. New York: Dutton, 1965.
3118. Ungainly things. New York: Dutton, 1968.

WALSH, Chad
3119. The factual dark. Prairie City, IL: Decker, 1949.
3120. Eden two-way. New York: Harper, 1954.
3121. The psalm of Christ. Philadelphia: Westminster, 1964.
3122. The unknowing dance. London and New York: Abelard-Schuman, 1964.
3123. The end of nature. Chicago: Swallow, 1969.

WARREN, Robert Penn
3124. Thirty-six poems. New York: Alcestis, 1935.
3125. Eleven poems on the same theme. Norfolk, CT: New Directions, 1942.
3126. Selected poems, 1923-43. New York: Harcourt, Brace, 1944.
3127. Brother to dragons, a tale in verse and voices. New York: Random House, 1953.
3128. Promises; poems, 1954-1956. New York: Random House, 1957.
3129. You, emperors, and others: poems, 1957-1960. New York: Random House, 1960.
3130. Selected poems, new and old, 1923-1966. New York: Random House, 1966.
3131. Incarnations; poems, 1966-1968. New York: Random House, 1968.
3132. Audubon, a vision. New York: Random House, 1969.

WARSH, Lewis
3133. The suicide rates. Eugene, OR: Toad, 1967.
3134. Highjacking. New York: Boke, 1968.
3135. Moving through air. New York: Angel Hair, 1968.
3136. Dreaming as one. New York: Corinth, 1972.

WATSON, Robert
3137. A paper horse. New York: Atheneum, 1962.
3138. Advantages of dark. New York: Atheneum, 1966.
3139. Christmas in Las Vegas. New York: Atheneum, 1971.

WATSON, Wilfred
3140. Friday's child. London: Faber, 1955; New York: Farrar, Straus, 1956.

WATT, William Whyte
3141. One man's meter. New York: Rinehart, 1959.

WEATHERLY, Tom
3142. Main stem stuff; the brighter side of Broadway and Manhattan. New York: Library Publishers, 1954.
3143. Maumau American cantos. New York: Corinth, 1970.
3144. Thumbprint. Norwood, PA: Telegraph Books, 1973.

WEBER, Marc
   3145. 48 small poems. Pittsburgh: University of Pittsburgh
          Press, 1973.

WEEKS, Robert Lewis
   3146. For those who waked me, and other poems, 1964-1969.
          Fort Smith, AR: South and West, 1969.
   3147. A master of clouds. La Crosse, WI: Juniper, 1971.

WEIDMAN, Phil
   3148. 6ixes. Sacramento: Runcible Spoon, 1968.

WEIL, James L.
   3149. Logarhythms. New York: Poetry Library, 1956.
   3150. Quarrel with the rose. Cleveland: American Weave, 1958.
   3151. A fool turns clockwise. Cleveland: American Weave, 1960.
   3152. The oboe player. Francestown, NH: Golden Quill, 1961.
   3153. Sorrow's spy. Cleveland: American Weave, 1963.
   3154. The thing said. Cleveland: American Weave, 1965.
   3155. The correspondences. Cleveland: American Weave, 1968.
   3156. There was. New Rochelle, NY: Elizabeth, 1969.
   3157. Un easy. New Rochelle, NY: Elizabeth, 1969.
   3158. To her hand. New Rochelle, NY: Elizabeth, 1973.
   3159. Your father. New Rochelle, NY: Elizabeth, 1973.

WEINFIELD, Henry
   3160. The carnival cantata. Santa Barbara: Unicorn, 1971.

WEISS, Theodore
   3161. The catch. New York: Twayne, 1951.
   3162. Outlanders. New York: Macmillan, 1960.
   3163. Gunsight. New York: New York University Press, 1962.
   3164. The medium. New York: Macmillan, 1965.
   3165. The last day and the first. New York: Macmillan, 1968.
   3166. The world before us; poems, 1950-70. New York: Macmillan, 1970.

WELCH, James
   3167. Riding the Earthboy 40. New York: World, 1971.

WELCH, Lew
   3168. Wobbly rock. San Francisco: Auerhahn, 1960.
   3169. Hermit poems. San Francisco: Four Seasons, 1965.
   3170. On out. Berkeley: Oyez, 1965.
   3171. The song my Tamalpais sings. Berkeley: Sand Dollar, 1971.

3172. Ring of bone: collected poems, 1950-1971. Bolinas,
      CA: Grey Fox, 1973.

WEST, John Foster
3173. Up ego! New York: Payton, Paul, 1951.

WHALEN, Philip
3174. Three satires. Portland, OR: privately printed, 1951.
3175. Like I say. New York: Totem, 1960.
3176. Memoirs of an interglacial age. San Francisco:
      Coyote, 1960.
3177. Monday in the evening. Milan: 263 Milano, 1964.
3178. Every day. Eugene, OR: Coyote's Journal, 1965.
3179. Highgrade; doodles, poems. Eugene, OR: Coyote's
      Journal, 1966.
3180. The education continues along. Eugene, OR: Toad,
      1967.
3181. Braincandy. New York: Poets Press, a. 1969.
3182. On Bear's Head. New York: Harcourt, Brace, 1969.
3183. Severance pay; poems, 1967-1969. San Francisco:
      Four Seasons, 1970.
3184. Scenes of life at the capital. Bolinas, CA: Grey Fox,
      1971.
3185. Imaginary speeches for a brazen head. Los Angeles:
      Black Sparrow, 1972.

WHEATCROFT, John
3186. Death of a clown. New York: T. Yoseloff, 1964.
3187. Prodigal son. New York: T. Yoseloff, 1967.

WHITBREAD, Thomas
3188. Four infinitives. New York: Harper & Row, 1964.

WHITE, James L.
3189. Divorce proceedings. Vermillion: University of South
      Dakota Press, 1972.

WHITEHEAD, James
3190. Domains. Baton Rouge: Louisiana State University
      Press, 1966.

WHITMAN, Ruth
3191. Blood and milk poems. New York: Clarke and Way,
      1963.
3192. The marriage wig, and other poems. New York:
      Harcourt, Brace, 1968.
3193. The passions of Lizzie Borden. New York: October
      House, 1972.

WHITNEY, J. D.
3194. Tracks. New Rochelle, NY: Elizabeth, 1969.
3195. The Nabisco warehouse. New Rochelle, NY: Elizabeth,
      1971.

WHITTEMORE, Reed
3196. Heroes and heroines. New York: Reynal and Hitch-
cock, 1947.
3197. An American takes a walk, and other poems. Minne-
apolis: University of Minnesota Press, 1956.
3198. The self-made man, and other poems. New York:
Macmillan, 1959.
3199. The boy from Iowa. New York: Macmillan, 1962.
3200. The fascination of the abomination. New York: Mac-
millan, 1963.
3201. Poems, new and selected. Minneapolis: University of
Minnesota Press, 1967.
3202. From zero to the absolute. New York: Crown, 1968.
3203. Fifty poems fifty. Minneapolis: University of Minne-
sota Press, 1970.

WIEDER, Laurance
3204. The coronet of tours. Ithaca, NY: Ithaca House, 1972.

WIENERS, John
3205. The Hotel Wentley poems. San Francisco: Auerhahn,
1958; rev. ed., 1966.
3206. Ace of pentacles. New York: J. F. Carr, 1964.
3207. Gardenias. New York: Phoenix Books, 1964.
3208. Pressed wafer. Buffalo, NY: Gallery Upstairs, 1968.
3209. Selected poems. London: Cape, 1968.
3210. Asylum poems. New York: Angel Hair, 1969.
3211. Nerves. London: Cape Goliard, 1970.
3212. Selected poems. New York: Grossman, 1972.

WIGGAM, Lionel
3213. The land of unloving. New York: Macmillan, 1961.

WILBUR, Richard
3214. Ceremony, and other poems. New York: Harcourt,
Brace, 1950.
3215. The beautiful changes, and other poems. New York:
Harcourt, Brace, 1954.
3216. Things of this world. New York: Harcourt, Brace,
1956.
3217. Poems, 1943-56. London: Faber, 1957.
3218. Advice to a prophet, and other poems. New York:
Harcourt, Brace, 1961.
3219. The poems of Richard Wilbur. New York: Harcourt,
Brace, 1963.
3220. Complaint. New York: Phoenix Book Shop, 1968.
3221. Walking to sleep. New York: Harcourt, Brace, 1969.
3222. Digging for China. Garden City, NY: Doubleday, 1970.
3223. Opposites. New York: Harcourt, Brace, 1973.

WILD, Peter
3224. Aragon. Monterey, CA: Polygon, 1967.
3225. The good fox. Glassboro, NJ: Goodly, 1967.

3226. The afternoon in dismay. Cincinnati: Art Association
of Cincinnati, 1968.
3227. Joining up & other poems. Sacramento: Runcible
Spoon, 1968.
3228. Mad night with sunflowers. Sacramento: Runcible
Spoon, 1968.
3229. Mica mountain poems. Northwood Narrows, NH:
Lillabulero, 1968.
3230. Sonnets. San Francisco: Cranium, 1968.
3231. Love poems. Northwood Narrows, NH: Lillabulero,
1969.
3232. Three nights in the Chiricahuas. Madison, WI:
Abraxas, 1969.
3233. Fat man poems. Belmont, MA: Hellric, 1970.
3234. Terms & renewals. San Francisco: Twowindows,
1970.
3235. Peligros. Ithaca, NY: Ithaca House, 1971.
3236. Wild's magical book of cranial effusions. New York:
New Rivers, 1971.
3237. Cochise. Garden City, NY: Doubleday, 1973.
3238. New and selected poems. New York: New Rivers,
1973.

WILKINSON, R. T.
3239. Survivors. Ithaca, NY: Stone Marrow, 1971.

WILL, Frederic
3240. Mosaic, and other poems. University Park: Pennsyl-
vania State University Press, 1959.
3241. A wedge of words. Austin: University of Texas Press,
1962.
3242. Planets. Francestown, NH: Golden Quill, 1966.
3243. Brandy in the snow. New York: New Rivers, 1972.
3244. Guatemala. Binghamton, NY: Bellevue, 1973.

WILLARD, Nancy
3245. In his country. Ann Arbor, MI: Generation, 1966.
3246. Skin of grace. Columbia: University of Missouri
Press, 1967.
3247. A new herball. Baltimore: Ferdinand Roten Galleries,
1968.
3248. 19 masks for a naked poet. Santa Cruz, CA: Kayak,
1971.

WILLIAMS, C. K.
3249. A day for Anne Frank. Philadelphia: Falcon, 1968.
3250. Lies. Boston: Houghton Mifflin, 1969.
3251. I am the bitter name. Boston: Houghton Mifflin, 1972.

WILLIAMS, Emmett
3252. The last french fried potato, and other poems. New
York: Something Else, 1967.
3253. Sweethearts. Barton, VT: Something Else, 1967.

3254. Selected shorter poems. Barton, VT: Something Else, 1973.
3255. A Valentine for Noel. Barton, VT: Something Else, 1973.

WILLIAMS, Gil
3256. Moving on. Binghamton, NY: Bellevue, 1973.

WILLIAMS, Jonathan
3257. Red/Gray. Highlands, NC: Jargon, 1951.
3258. Four stoppages; a configuration, verse. Stuttgart, 1953.
3259. The empire finals at Verona. Highlands, NC: Jargon, 1959.
3260. Amen/Huzza/Selah. Highlands, NC: Jargon, 1961.
3261. Elegies and celebrations. Highlands, NC: Jargon, 1962.
3262. In England's green & (a garland and a clyster). San Francisco: Auerhahn, 1962.
3263. Lullabies, twisters, gibbers, drags. Highlands, NC: Nantahala, 1963.
3264. Affilati Attrezzi per i giardini di Catullo. Milan: Lerici Editore, 1967.
3265. Fifty epiphytes. London: Poet and Printer, 1967.
3266. Mahler becomes politics... Beisbol. London: Marlborough Gallery, 1967.
3267. Descant on Rawthey's madrigal. Lexington, KY: Gnomen, 1968.
3268. The lucidities. London: Turret Books, 1968.
3269. Sharp tools for Catullan gardens. Bloomington: Indiana University Fine Arts Department, 1968.
3270. An ear in Bartram's tree; selected poems, 1957-1967. Chapel Hill: University of North Carolina Press, 1969; New York: New Directions, 1972.
3271. The apocryphal, oracular yeah-sayings of Mae West. Baltimore: Institute of Art, 1969.
3272. Mahler. London: Cape Goliard, 1969.
3273. The new architectural monuments of Baltimore city. Baltimore: Institute of Art, 1969.
3274. Six rusticated, wall-eyed poems. Baltimore: Maryland Institute of Art, 1969.
3275. Strung out with Elgar on a hill. Urbana, IL: Finial, 1969.
3276. Excavations from the case histories of Havelock Ellis. London: Turret Books, 1970.
3277. The plastic hydrangea people poems. London: Marlborough Gallery, 1970.
3278. Blues & roots, rue & bluets; a garland for the Appalachians. New York: Grossman, 1971.
3279. The loco logodaedalist in situ; selected poems, 1968-1970. New York: Cape Goliard, 1972.
3280. Imaginary postcards. London: Trigram, 1973.

WILLIAMS, Miller
    3281. Letters to the editor, and other poems. New York:
          Pageant, 1955.
    3282. A circle of stone. Baton Rouge: Louisiana State Uni-
          versity Press, 1964.
    3283. So long at the fair. New York: Dutton, 1968.
    3284. The only world there is. New York: Dutton, 1971.

WILLIAMS, Mona
    3285. Voices in the dark. Garden City, NY: Doubleday,
          1968.

WILLIAMS, Oscar
    3286. The golden darkness. New Haven: Yale University
          Press, 1921.
    3287. Selected poems. New York: Clarke & Way, 1958.
    3288. Selected poems. New York: October House, 1964.

WILLS, Jesse
    3289. Early and late. Nashville: Vanderbilt University
          Press, 1959.

WILSON, Keith
    3290. The old car & other black poems. Sacramento:
          Grande Ronde, 1967.
    3291. Sketches for a New Mexico hill town. Concord, MA:
          Wine, 1967.
    3292. Lion's gate. New York: Grove, 1968.
    3293. II sequences. Portland, OR: Wine, 1968.
    3294. Graves registry, and other poems. New York: Grove,
          1969.
    3295. Homestead. San Francisco: Kayak, 1969.
    3296. The old man & others; some faces for America. Uni-
          versity Park: New Mexico State University Press,
          1970.
    3297. The shadow of our bones. Portland, OR: Trask
          House, 1970.
    3298. Midwatch. Fremont, MI: Sumac, 1972.

WINSLOW, Pete
    3299. Monster cookies. San Francisco: privately printed,
          1966.
    3300. A daisy in the memory of a shark. San Francisco:
          City Lights, 1973.

WINTERS, Yvor
    3301. The immobile wind. Evanston, IL: M. Wheeler, 1921.
    3302. The bare hills. Boston: Four Seas, 1927.
    3303. The proof. New York: Coward-McCann, 1930.
    3304. Before disaster. Tryon, NC: Tryon Pamphlets, 1934.
    3305. Poems. Los Altos, CA: Gyroscope, 1940.
    3306. The giant weapon. Norfolk, CT: New Directions, 1943.
    3307. Three poems. Cummington, MA: Cummington, 1950.

3308. Collected poems. Denver: Swallow, 1952; rev., 1960.
3309. The brink of darkness. 1965.
3310. The early poems of Yvor Winters, 1920-28. Denver: Swallow, 1966.

WITHERUP, William
3311. Sangre de Cristo Mountain poems. Northwood Narrows, NH: Lillabulero, 1970.

WITT, Harold
3312. Beasts in clothes. New York: Macmillan, 1961.
3313. Pop. by 1940: 40,000. Crete, NE: Best Cellar, 1971.

WOESSNER, Warren
3314. The forest and the trees. Madison, WI: Quixote, 1968.
3315. The rivers return. Milwaukee: Gunrunner, 1969.
3316. Inroads. Madison, WI: Modine Gunch, 1970.
3317. Cross-country. Madison, WI: Quest, 1972.

WOLDE, Habte (Henry Jennings)
3318. Enough to die for. Detroit: Broadside, 1972.

WOLFERT, Helen
3319. The music. New York: Norton, 1965.

WONG, May
3320. A bad girl's book of animals. New York: Harcourt, Brace, 1969.
3321. Reports. New York: Harcourt, Brace, 1972.

WOOD, William Parker
3322. The shrinking orchestra. New York: Macmillan, 1963.

WOODS, John
3323. The deaths at Paragon, Indiana. Bloomington: Indiana University Press, 1955.
3324. On the morning of color. Bloomington: Indiana University Press, 1961.
3325. The cutting edge. Bloomington: Indiana University Press, 1966.
3326. Keeping out of trouble. Bloomington: Indiana University Press, 1968.
3327. Turning to look back; poems, 1955-1970. Bloomington: Indiana University Press, 1972.

WRIGHT, Celeste Turner
3328. Etruscan princess, and other poems. Denver: Swallow, 1964.

WRIGHT, Charles
3329. Private madrigals. Madison, WI: Abraxas, 1969.
3330. The grave of the right hand. Middletown, CT: Wesleyan University Press, 1970.

3331. The venice notebook. Boston: Barn Dream, 1971.
3332. Hard freight. Middletown, CT: Wesleyan University Press, 1973.

WRIGHT, Charles David
   3333. Early rising. Chapel Hill: University of North Carolina Press, 1968.

WRIGHT, James
   3334. The green wall. New Haven: Yale University Press, 1957.
   3335. Saint Judas. Middletown, CT: Wesleyan University Press, 1959.
   3336. The branch will not break. Middletown, CT: Wesleyan University Press, 1963.
   3337. Shall we gather at the river. Middletown, CT: Wesleyan University Press, 1968.
   3338. Collected poems. Middletown, CT: Wesleyan University Press, 1971.
   3339. Two citizens. New York: Farrar, Straus, 1973.

WRIGHT, Jay
   3340. The homecoming singer. New York: Corinth, 1971.

WYATT, Andrea
   3341. Three rooms. Berkeley: Oyez, 1970.
   3342. Poems of the morning & poems of the storm. Berkeley: Oyez, 1972.

WYLIE, Andrew
   3343. Gold. Norwood, PA: Telegraph Books, 1973.

X, Marvin (El Muhajir; Marvin Jackmon)
   3344. Fly to Allah. Fresno, CA: Al Kitab Sudan, 1969.
   3345. Black man listen. Detroit: Broadside, 1970.

YELLEN, Samuel
   3346. In the house and out, and other poems. Bloomington: Indiana University Press, 1952.
   3347. New & selected poems. Bloomington: Indiana University Press, 1964.
   3348. The convex mirror; collected poems. Bloomington: Indiana University Press, 1971.

YOUNG, Al
   3349. Dancing. New York: Corinth, 1969.
   3350. The song turning back into itself. New York: Holt, Rinehart and Winston, 1971.

YOUNG, David P.
3351. Six poems from Wang Weo. Oberlin, OH: Triskelion, 1969.
3352. Sweating out the winter. Pittsburgh: University of Pittsburgh Press, 1969.
3353. Thoughts of Chairman Mao. Oberlin, OH: Triskelion, 1970.

YOUNG, Jim
3354. Take it with you. Crete, NE: Best Cellar, 1973.

ZATURENSKA, Marya
3355. Threshold and hearth. New York: Macmillan, 1934.
3356. Cold morning sky. New York: Macmillan, 1937.
3357. The listening landscape. New York: Macmillan, 1941.
3358. Golden Mirror. New York: Macmillan, 1944.
3359. Selected poems. New York: Grove, 1954.
3360. Terraces of light. New York: Grove, 1960.
3361. Collected poems. New York: Viking, 1965.

ZEKOWSKI, Arlene
3362. Seasons of the mind. New York: Wittenborn, 1969.

ZIMMER, Paul
3363. A seed on the wind. San Francisco: privately printed, 1960.
3364. The ribs of death. New York: October House, 1967.
3365. The republic of many voices. New York: October House, 1969.

ZUKOFSKY, Louis
3366. Fifty-five poems. Prairie City, IL: Decker, 1941.
3367. Anew. Prairie City, IL: Decker, 1946.
3368. Some Time. Highlands, NC: Jargon, 1956.
3369. Barely and widely. New York: C. Zukofsky, 1958.
3370. "A" 1-12. Ashland, MA: Origin, and Kyoto: Origin, 1959; London: Jonathan Cape, 1966; New York: Doubleday, and Paris Review eds., 1967.
3371. After I's. Pittsburgh: Boxwood, 1964.
3372. All the collected short poems, 1923-1958. New York: Norton, 1965; London: Jonathan Cape, 1966.
3373. Iyyob. London: Turret, 1965.
3374. All the collected short poems, 1956-1964. New York: Norton, 1966; London: Jonathan Cape, 1967.
3375. Prepositions. London: Rapp & Carroll, 1967.
3376. "A" 13-21. Garden City, NY: Doubleday, and London: Jonathan Cape, 1969.
3377. Initial. New York: Phoenix Book Shop, 1970.
3378. Little. New York: Grossman, 1970.
3379. All the collected short poems, 1923-1964. New York: Norton, 1971.

3380. "A" 24. New York: Grossman, 1972.

ZWEIG, Paul
    3381. Against emptiness. New York: Harper & Row, 1971.

TITLE INDEX

139

Hurrah for anything. 2323
The hurricane lamp. 43
Hymn to the gentle sun. 1652
Hymns to St. Geryon, and
   other poems. 1858

I advance with loaded rose. 277
I am a Black woman. 949
I am! says the lamb. 2552
I am the babe of Joseph Stalin's
   daughter; poems, 1961-1971.
   2281
I am the bitter name. 3251
I counted only April. 2345
I marry you; a sheaf of love
   poems. 497
I met a man. 499
I remember. 324
I remember the room was
   filled with light. 1296
I went to see my true love.
   1647
Iconographs. 2925
Icy rose. 3104
Idaho out. 771
Identikit. 353
Identities. 2109
If madness were bred. 1496
If personal. 2693
If you. 636
Ikabana. 2500
I'll be home late tonight. 1846
I'm a stranger here myself.
   2128
The image and the law. 2171
Imaginary postcards. 3280
Imaginary speeches for a brazen
   head. 3185
Imaginative qualities of actual
   things. 2821
Imitations. 1828
The immaculate. 1549
The immobile wind. 3301
The immoral proposition. 637
Imperatives. 2277
Impossible buildings. 2750
In a time between wars. 1543
In advance of the broken arm.
   2288
In advent. 2425
In America. 292

In an iridescent time. 2882
In an ordinary place. 2443
In cold hell, in thicket. 2231
In defense of the earth. 2490
In defiance of the rain. 1046
In dreams begin responsibilities.
   2687
In easy dark. 145
In England's green & (a garland
   and a clyster). 3262
In fact. 502
In good time. 578
In his country. 3245
In London. 649
In memory of my feelings; a se-
   lection of poems. 2223
In Mexico. 2917
In my Father's house. 1160
In narrow bound. 2842
In no time. 579
In. on. or about the premises. 269
In open woods. 2751
In praise of Adam. 727
In quest of candlelighters. 2337
In quire. 2297
In the cold country. 1402
In the deepest aquarium. 2812
In the early morning rain. 218
In the fictive wish. 77
In the financial district. 2420
In the furrows of the world. 528
In the heart of our city. 2586
In the house and out, and other
   poems. 3346
In the Mecca. 371
In the outer dark. 2402
In the rose of time, poems 1931-
   1956. 1004
In the silent stones. 2482
In the stoneworks. 500
In the temperate zone. 1671
In the terrified radiance. 431
In this corner. 600
In this place. 302
In time. 1584
In time like air. 2649
In time; poems, 1962-1968. 2263
In what hour. 2485
Incarnations; poems, 1966-1968.
   3131
Indian mountain. 402
Indian territory and other poems.
   3022

through life and expiate all
that's been sadly done. 619
There was. 3156
There's a little ambiguity over
there among the bluebells,
and other theater poems.
1662
There's always a moon in
America. 1000
There's always another wind-
mill. 2156
These are the ravens. 61
These islands also. 1469
Theseus and other poems. 406
They feed they lion. 1769
The thicket of spring; poems,
1926-1969. 314
Thing of sorrow. 2242
The thing said. 3154
Things of this world. 3216
Things we dreamt we died for.
178
Think black. 1738
Thirteen mad sonnets. 1862
Thirty epigrams. 2211
39 poems (Ciardi). 498
Thirty one sonnets. 850
Thirty-seven poems: one night
stanzas. 2338
Thirty-six poems (Warren). 3124
33 night sonnets. 538
33 phases of the fatal strobo-
scope. 2054
This. 2230
This breast gothic. 1664
This do & the talents. 911
This element. 2927
This in which. 2253
This kind of bird flies backward.
753
This lonely house. 2072
This strangest everything. 505
This time, that space. 1021
This world. 2730
Thistles. 1766
Thomas Merton: early poems/
1940-42. 2017
Thorns and thistles. 2122
Though gently. 2522
Thought. 1732
Thoughts of Chairman Mao.
3353
The thousand and second night.

2005
Thousand-year-old fiancée. 2916
Threads (Bartlett). 157
Threads (Bromige). 358
"3. " 451
Three ages of lake light. 2571
Three nights in the Chiricahuas.
3232
Three on fire. 477
3 or 4 poems about the sea.
1733
Three poems (Ashbery). 102
Three poems (Eberhart). 852
Three poems (Merwin). 2024
Three poems (Winters). 3307
3 poems for Benedetta Barzini.
1936
Three priests in April. 2859
Three rooms. 3341
Three satires. 3174
Three years rings. 2352
Threshold and hearth. 3355
Through the woods. 90
Thumbprint. 3144
Thursdays and every other Sunday
off. 1193
Tidings, poems at the land's
edge. 386
Time is our house. 1918
A time of bees. 3029
A time of black devotion. 1606
A time of turning. 784
Time raid. 3014
Time without number. 204
Time's web. 2089
The tin can, and other poems.
2791
Titled and untitled. 1023
Tlateloco: a sequence from Que.
2507
To a high place. 2657
To a new husband. 2622
To be of use. 2381
To Bedlam and part way back.
2715
To come to have become. 912
To construct a clock. 2929
To Corrado Cagli. 2227
To face the sea. 765
To flower. 697
To her hand. 3158
To keep the house from falling
in. 686

What friends are for. 1688
What I want. 1048
What the grass says. 2758
Whatever love declares. 1596
The wheel age. 427
The wheel of summer. 1706
Wheels of light. 1940
When children played as kings
   and queens. 2810
When the sun tries to go on.
   1639
When thy king is a boy. 2534
When we were here together.
   2324
Where I hang my hat. 1069
Where is all the music? 948
Where is Vietnam? 977
Where the bone is green. 1295
Where the compass spins. 2830
Where the ocean covers us. 1945
Where we are. 608
The whip. 638
White. 2761
The white bird. 2843
White blossoms. 2039
White country. 2673
Which hand holds the brother;
   poems, 1966-1968. 2347
Whistling in the labyrinth. 391
White-haired lover. 2741
White lights and whale hearts.
   3051
White paper. 2854
The white stallion, and other
   poems. 2278
White sun black sun. 2572
Who is she that looketh forth
   as the morning. 83
Who look at me. 1517
Whole horse. 2564
Wichita vortex sutra. 1118
The wild anemone. 1719
Wild-craft. 2394
Wild flowers out of gas. 479
Wild lace. 2536
The wilderness, and other
   poems. 629
Wilderness of ladies. 2954
Wilderness stair. 172
Wild's magical book of cranial
   effusions. 3236
The will of Eros; selected poems
   1930-1970. 3003

The will to change; poems 1968-
   1970. 2516
Willamette. 2545
William Blake. 1331
William Stafford: eleven untitled
   poems. 2837
The wind southerly. 2058
Windfall. 28
A windmill near Calvary. 3106
A window for New York. 2445
The window. 2607
The winds of the calendar. 1898
Wine. 810
A winter come, a summer gone;
   poems 1946-1960. 2113
Winter insomnia. 468
The winter lightning; selected
   poems. 2178
Winter news. 1205
Winter trees. 2401
Winters. 604
Winterward. 2833
The wishing animal. 722
With boards & old postcards in-
   side us. 1780
With eyes at the back of our
   heads. 1753
With light reflected. 925
A witness to the times. 1888
Wobbly rock. 3168
The woman at the Washington
   Zoo. 1481
The woman from the island. 1468
A woman unashamed, and other
   poems. 904
The woman who loved worms and
   other poems. 1467
Women in love, and other poems.
   2204
Wondering where you are. 2369
Wonderstrand revisited, a Cape
   Cod sequence. 2375
Woo havoc. 181
The wooden horse. 1321
Word alchemy. 1540
Word from the hills: a sonnet
   sequence in 4 movements. 2087
The word of love. 898
Words. 643
Words and photographs. 2642
Words for each other. 587
Words for the wind. 2551
Words in the mourning time. 1272